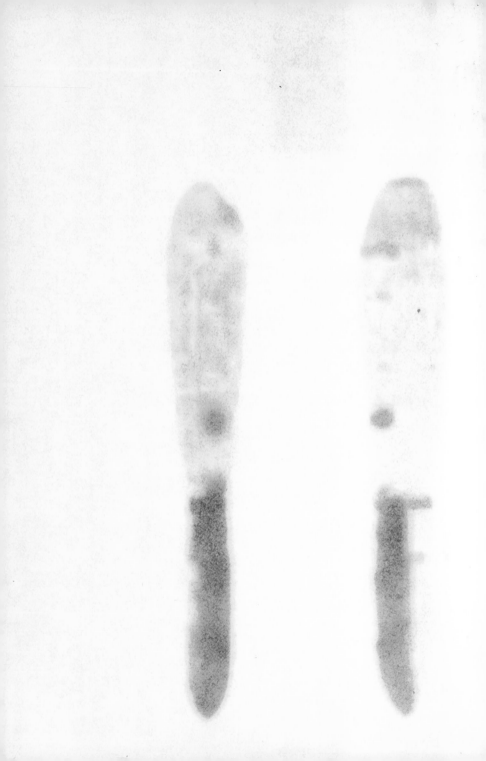

COMMUNICATE

Parkinson's Formula
for Business Survival

COMMUNICATE

Parkinson's Formula

for Business Survival

C. NORTHCOTE PARKINSON

and

NIGEL ROWE

Prentice/Hall   PHI   International

Englewood Cliffs, New Jersey

First published in the United States of America, 1978

© **1977 by Prentice-Hall International, Inc.**

ISBN 0-13-153460-2

10 9 8 7 6 5 4 3 2

Printed in the United States of America.

Prentice-Hall International, Inc., *London*
Prentice-Hall of Australia Pty. Ltd., *Sydney*
Prentice-Hall of Canada, Ltd., *Toronto*
Prentice-Hall of India Private Limited, *New Delhi*
Prentice-Hall of of Japan, Inc., *Tokyo*
Prentice-Hall of Southeast Asia Pte., Ltd., *Singapore*
Prentice-Hall, Inc., *Englewood Cliffs, New Jersey*
Whitehall Books Limited, *Wellington, New Zealand*

Contents

Foreword
by Peter F. Drucker

Businessmen – in Europe perhaps even more than in the United States – constantly complain about the public's "hostility to business". But the real danger to business and to the survival of a free economy is not hostility to business. It is the total lack of understanding what business is, what business does, what businessmen are and what businessmen do. To be sure, there are plenty of enemies of business and of the free economy. But they are successful primarily because the rest of the public does not understand what the debate is all about, does not understand what business does and what it contributes, what business can do and what it cannot do, and above all why business behaves the way it does. And so a public, which by no means shares the beliefs of the enemies of business, goes along with their proposed policies and laws simply because it lacks the understanding to oppose what in the long run then always turns out to be detrimental to the very public that supports – or at least accepts – the laws and regulations and measures proposed by the enemies of business.

This lack of understanding is by no means confined to the "intellectuals" or the "students" or to the public outside altogether. It begins within business. It begins just below the top management level. The engineer in the company's research department understands, as a rule, no more about business than do the professors of English or of Sociology or their students. It is a general lack of understanding. And no one is responsible for it except the businessman. For what business is and what business does are not particularly mysterious. It does not take a great deal of intelligence or advanced education to understand that there really is no such thing as "profit". There are only "costs of the past" and "costs of the future". What is called "profit" is, in part, the insurance premiums for the risks of uncertainty which committing present-day resources to the future always implies. It is in part the needed capital to finance and create the jobs of tomorrow. And then, of course, increasingly what we call "profit" is in effect the cost of all the non-economic activities of society – from the opera and the art museum to the schools and the government agencies. People find this very easy to understand. But nobody ever says it, or says it in a form in which ordinary laymen can grasp and understand a simple proposition.

This is clearly the fault of the businessman. It is perhaps not that he says the wrong things – although very often he does (for instance, when he talks of profit maximization or profit motive). It is simply that he does not realize that what is so obvious to him nobody else can see at all. Yet this is the first rule of psychology. To be understood, one has to make oneself understood. Nobody understands anybody else unless there is a serious and organized attempt to convey understanding. Nobody understands unless there is a serious and organized attempt to communicate.

In this new book, Professor C. Northcote Parkinson and Mr. Nigel Rowe attempt to enable the businessman to communicate. Of course, there are hundreds of books on business communications. But I do not know of any other which understands the basic rules of rhetoric, I do not know of any other which understands what is needed for effective communication. Effective communication has four parts – something we have known since Plato and Aristotle – only our businessmen seem never to have heard of it. One has to know what to say; one has to know when to say it; one has to know to whom to say it; and one has to know how to say it. If one of those four elements is missing, there cannot be communication. And this book, to my knowledge for the first time, tackles all four elements of communication. It makes the businessman literate and it gives him the competence which he needs. It may be very late for this. The lack of understanding of business has created an environment in which business may not be able to survive – and in Europe even more so than in the United States. But it is not too late to tackle a job which business has had ever since the first large business emerged – that is ever since the businessman ceased to be "private" and became a visible public figure. I can only hope that many business leaders will read this book, will study it, will learn from it – and will then practice what Parkinson and Rowe so ably preach.

Claremont, California

Acknowledgements

Our thanks are due to Mike Wade for introducing us to each other in the first place; to Management Centre Europe (MCE), especially Clem Livingstone and Mike Johnson, for their very real assistance; to Nick Winkfield of Landell Mills Associates who designed and conducted the opinion research featured in Chapter 3, in co-operation with MCE, and to the more than 400 chief executives who participated in the project; to the more than fifty business leaders, business critics and others who gave freely of their time and opinions in personal interviews, many of whom are referred to in the text; to Philip Rosenthal, Jayne Baker Spain, Eric-Jan Tuininge, Brian Basham and Herbert Schmertz who have contributed case studies; and to our wives, Ann and Tove, whose long-suffering support sustained us throughout the project.

C.N.P.
N.R.

COMMUNICATE

Parkinson's Formula

for Business Survival

SECTION ONE

The business environment

1

Business Under Pressure

Popular fear and hostility towards industry are based to a large extent on a mistrust of the unknown – an ignorance of industry's limitations, achievements and contributions to society. When people are frightened of something, especially if the fear is irrational and based on ignorance, they want that something controlled – be it a large animal or a large corporation.

They do not want industry wandering the streets without a collar and lead.

Industry has either assumed a popular understanding and knowledge that does not exist, or else it has itself decided to ignore the ignorance. With the rise of socialism and communism, movements that threaten private enterprise and influence governments that are not avowedly left-wing, the businessman has been thrown on the defensive. He feels that all 'liberal' and enlightened opinion is against him and that his best plan is to avoid publicity. His case has gone by default and he has been condemned without a hearing. He may conclude – he often does – that his work is difficult enough in itself without adding to it the task of continual explanation. With that view any fair commentator must sympathize, and yet the fact remains that this explanation must be provided by someone. The work being done is of interest to government (both central and local), to the financial community, to the shareholders, to the company's workers, to the trade unions and to the press. What the industrialist may refuse to disclose a lot of other people are ready to reveal, distort and invent. Where there are no flowers there will often be plenty of weeds.

But if the desire to communicate and some technical knowledge of the means of communication are present, attempts to convey a message will be frustrated if the difference between merely *transmitting* and actually *communicating* a message is not understood – the latter requiring implicitly that the message be received, comprehended and even accepted. The story is told of British Prime Minister Benjamin Disraeli telling Queen Victoria, with obvious emotion: 'Your Majesty, I am proud to announce that through a great feat of technology the electric telegraph now links London with the continent of India, and your Majesty's government is now able to communicate directly and promptly with the peoples of India.' Queen Victoria is said to have pondered this news for a moment before replying: 'I dare say, Mr Prime Minister, but what of relevance does my government have to *say* to my subjects in India?'

We need also to realize that criticism is largely, though not entirely, directed against the larger companies and especially against those that are multinational in character. Critics fail to notice the merits of these large organizations, and are quick to comment on the rare (but much publicized) instances of their intervention in politics and perceived abuses of power. Nor are these criticisms to be ignored. There is, in effect, a case to answer.

Behind this case lie two general considerations. First of all, the development of democratic institutions has latterly ensured the election to high office of men whose origins are relatively humble and whose means are relatively modest. The result has been to place political power in the hands of men who are without personal fortune. The politician may thus be brought into social contact with men of wealth and family interest, creating the perfect background for corruption. Rumour (often baseless) suggests that politician A is on the secret payroll of corporation B which is to benefit from concessions, contracts and permits, and public opinion is apt to blame the corporation more than the politician. This type of corruption now overlays and adds to the type that involves those who already have wealth, vested interest and position to protect.

In the second place, it becomes difficult to defend the larger corporations as examples of free enterprise. Where there is a conflict between a nation state and a small-scale manufacturer, the public might sympathize with the underdog. But the big corporation attracts less sympathy and is often the target of abuse on two counts (apart from political corruption).

1. The corporation is often regarded as the foe to free enterprise, the whale that swallows the minnows, the organization into which the smaller companies are absorbed.

2. The corporation is accused of practising monopoly, securing control of the market and fixing prices to its own advantage.

Big is not necessarily seen to be beautiful, though most managers with experience know that with a few well publicized exceptions the big corporations are more or less guiltless on either charge.

Where companies in general are perhaps more vulnerable is in such matters as pollution. There are forms of pollution that fall outside the scope of national legislation and have not so far been made the subject of any effective international agreement. It should be remembered, however, that nations and cities have just as bad a record where pollution is concerned. This would seem to be a matter in which the big corporations should agree among themselves to set a good example instead of following a bad one.

We must also consider two other important, and apparently conflicting, factors that have contributed towards public suspicion of business enterprise: education and ignorance. Until World War II, popular education in most countries was largely limited to basic literacy and numeracy. Further, it strongly underpinned such concepts as the Christian work ethic and respect for authority. Postwar education has expanded in two directions – the school-leaving age has been raised, and the process of education, especially state education, has been the subject of considerable experiment. Young people have been encouraged to develop personal aspirations that reality does not, and in many cases cannot, meet. Many young people emerge from the system with a confusion of wants. They insist that industry must provide full employment for all; but claim that work is degrading and boring. They insist that industry and technology have created problems like pollution and depletion of the world's natural resources; yet they expect industry to provide a continual increase in their standard of living, and creature comforts that only technology can provide. Ignorance is a factor that we referred to at the very beginning of this chapter – the popular ignorance of industry's limitations, achievements and contributions to society, an ignorance that has created widespread mistrust, fear and hostility towards business enterprise and a political need to 'control' industry.

All of these factors call for a strong, urgent and perhaps even aggressive response by business and industry. This is especially true in Europe, where the inherent threat to the survival of business enterprise is now immediate. But it is in contrast with the communication requirements implicit in one final area in which the corporation is under considerable pressure: worker participation, or industrial democracy.

To the public at large it may seem reasonable that workers should have some right to influence the companies on which they may depend for their livelihood. It can be argued that the modern working man will have had some form of secondary education and that his right to vote in a parliamentary election might well be parallelled by his right to appoint his representatives to his company's board of directors.

Industrial democracy exists, and indeed works fairly well, in almost half of Europe. Strike and inflation rates, and the relative effects of the recent economic recession, bear witness to this. Too frequently, however, worker participation is confused with worker control – or, worse, trade union control. This misrepresentation of the emerging form of European industrial democracy has given rise to considerable confusion in Britain and southern Europe, creating popular aspirations under the guise of worker participation that are more properly associated with the myth of collectivism and communism.

It is easy to forget the simple truth that industrial democracy depends upon the harmonization of the interests of industrial ownership, of those who contribute their labour (management and shopfloor worker), and of that element of society that conditions the context of our personal and corporate lives (government). Harmony requires sensible balance. It also, as a consequence, requires a type of communication that is unrelated to the assertive requirements of the front-line defence of business enterprise called for earlier in this chapter.

THE BUSINESSMAN'S CASE

In a world where so many people have theories about how money should be spent, however, and where he is the only one who seems to know how money is to be made, the businessman is in a stronger position than he is often able to grasp. His work, if successful, brings satisfaction to a vast number of people. The social worker takes money from A via taxation in order to give cocoa and advice to B, being rewarded by A's resentment and B's ingratitude. The industrialist buys his raw materials from A, borrows his capital from B, obtains a short-term loan from C, offers work at a fair salary or wage to his employees D to S, places his advertisements through the agency of T, loads his products on the trucks supplied by U, allows a commission to the wholesaler V and the retailer W, pays his taxes to collector Y and then uses his profit to repay C, provide a dividend for B and finally have something for himself, Z. At the end of a complex and often risky operation everyone is satisfied, not forgetting the bank manager, the tax collector, the insurance agent and the customer who has finally bought the product, whether a tractor, a pork pie or a ball-point pen. People have had fair payment for their services, and the goods (we hope) have been delivered on time. It is a transaction that satisfies all and does no possible harm to anyone. This is the *normal* course of business. So the businessman has some reason to think that he deserves more respect than he often receives.

Knowing the importance of his work, the industrialist is not easily shaken by ill-informed criticism. He is not always aware, however, of the advantages he might have in argument. There are, in fact, three points on which he might, and should, insist. In the first place, he created the world in which we actually live. Books on history and political science tell us of constitutional progress and representative government, but our immediate surroundings were created in most important respects by businessmen rather than by politicians. In the second place, the businessman has this advantage: he is international in outlook, while his critics are mostly parochial. Raw materials may come from afar in one direction, the finished product going as far in another direction. The one transaction may involve a number of different countries, with problems explained in as many different languages. In the third place, the technological trend of the age is to replace both the traditional employer and his opponent, the traditional trade unionist artisan. The employer has turned into a professional manager, a technician or financial expert or sometimes even a scientist. The employee is no longer an unschooled working man with cloth cap and soiled overalls. The manager and the man on the shop floor are nearer to each other in social origin. In any case, the old contrasts between the board room and the factory have lost much of their sharpness.

If the manager fails to state his case it is not because he is of higher social origin but merely because he has other things to do. In a very real sense the company executive is now a different sort of man, an expert, a man (and, increasingly, a woman) who knows his trade. He has a case and one that he needs to publicize. In the situation as it exists today the industrialist can no longer afford to remain silent. The time has come to communicate.

2

Industrial Diplomacy

The man who is a professional in management may be an amateur in stating his case. Goodwill and sincerity are not enough. There was a time when a managing director might expect a certain deference from other businessmen, from civil servants, from newspapermen and still more from his own employees. He had inherited something of the sort of respect that was shown by the old-time labourer to the country squire. His visitors might be tongue-tied and hesitant, his men might be expected to touch their caps. But each generation represents a further remove from our agricultural background. Our sense of responsibility is progressively weakened and so is our respect for seniority. It used to be assumed that wisdom must derive from experience and age, but our present assumption is that age goes with obsolescence, that the older man has not been on the computer course and that his experience is no longer applicable to the current problem. There is nothing to stop the senior man from showing that he is fully abreast of everything and is better qualified than anyone else, but he needs to prove it – it will not be generally assumed that he knows best. More than that, there are those among the youth of today whose prejudice is against the old as such. Their assumption is that the old must be wrong and that a man with a 'posh' accent must be a mere obstacle to progress. Those who speak for industry have a resistance to overcome. They may be given a hearing but they will not be given an unearned ovation.

If people at large have lost most of their respect for rank and age it is not necessarily because they have acquired a fiery resolve to think for themselves. Their literacy has exposed them to the influence of the press and of advertising. They are also influenced by the cassette and record player, by television and radio. The adulation once reserved for victorious admirals and distinguished generals, with some even to spare for judges and politicians, is now bestowed on singers, comedians and rebels. The general trend is against authority and age. When a public relations consultant talks to an industrialist about the need to communicate and develop a favourable reputation, he is sometimes told that a chief executive has other things to think about, that his concern is with results, not with popularity. What the chief executive fails to realize is that some sort of public image is in any case inevitable and that the image he will not create for himself will be created for him by other people and will not necessarily be to his advantage. To supersede the unfavourable image by one that will assist the smooth working of the organization – and that is nearer the truth – is not a simple or easy task. In an age when the public image of a leading politician is built up with the greatest care, the final picture being the work of consultants, photographers and journalists, we cannot expect fair treatment for an industrialist who confines himself to an occasional and laconic press release. To present the case for management is normally a task for the expert and not for the amateur. There have been instances, we know, when a chief executive has shown a flair for communication, but these have been more the exception than the rule. It is one thing to do the work, quite another to explain it to the public. Only rarely do we meet with anyone who can do both tasks equally well.

In past centuries the business of negotiation between different sovereign states was entrusted to professional diplomats, to men of a rather scholarly character who chose their words with caution and who knew each other extremely well. During the present century our diplomats have been pushed aside and we have heard of meetings in which the leading politicians of the different countries have been brought face to face, often with deplorable results. Skilled negotiation has given place to windy rhetoric and dramatic gesture, to imprecise agreement and subsequent recrimination. We may feel at times that the older style of diplomacy was more practical and, on average, more successful. Perhaps the same conclusion might be reached by a student of industrial and commercial policy. There would seem to be the need for an industrial diplomacy, an art of presenting the case for both national and multinational enterprise, as also of mediating between governments and companies. There are those who would ask what mediation should be needed between a sovereign state and an industrial corporation. They forget that a corporation can be larger, richer and more important than many a nation state, with branches spread over a continent and interests extended over the world. There is a growing need for industrial diplomacy, not that its exponents should conceal the facts, but rather that they should deny what is false and explain what they know to be true.

THE ART OF COMMUNICATION

When we begin to communicate, whether as a society or as individuals, our efforts are initially confused by our desire to express ourselves. We have an emotion and we want to give it an outlet. A lion roars (one would guess) because it feels like roaring, not because it has any profound thought to express. A dog barks without attempting to explain its philosophy or political outlook. We ourselves often express an emotion without any real purpose, save to unburden our minds of what we feel. When we drop a hammer on our toe we day 'Damn!' or 'Blast!' merely to relieve our feelings. Our exclamation does no good and may not even be heard by anyone else. We curse when we are alone. We complain about the cussedness of things – the door that jams, the tool that breaks, the screw that is lost, the light that fuses. The first thing to realize, therefore, is that most people want to talk but few of them have anything to say. Anyone who doubts this should watch someone in a glass-sided telephone kiosk. Note the gestures and expressions, the pointing finger, the clutched fist, the smile, the frown, the tapping foot. All these signs are wasted on the telephone. We realize, in fact, that they are not seriously meant to convey anything to anybody. They are means of self-expression and that is all. They are older than speech, and when the gesture contradicts the word, the gesture is more likely to be right. What is true of the individual is often as true of the organization. Those who sit in head offices may relieve their feelings in letters, telegrams, notices and memoranda, but these are often as meaningless as the gesture made when we are on the telephone. What people say or write or print often means nothing at all and is not even meant to mean anything. It is merely the bureaucratic equivalent of breaking wind.

Once we stop relieving our emotions and show the wish to communicate, there is a different situation altogether. Our feelings are set aside and we have a thought or wish or instruction to convey. We are now called upon to use our imagination. We have to visualize the person or persons we are seeking to influence. He may be – he often is – the man on the factory floor. We have to ask ourselves what he already knows, what he already believes (perhaps incorrectly), what his chief interests are, where he is likely to live and what newspaper (if any) he is likely to read. Does all this sound obvious? But it is far from obvious and is all too easily forgotten. Our basic mistake, eternally repeated, is to assume that what is known to us is known to everyone else.

If your directions are to be followed correctly, they must be explained clearly. There must be careful choice of words. Behind what is said there must be the wish to communicate. Behind the bad direction there is often a muddled motive: a desire to humiliate, a desire to reveal somebody's stupidity, a desire to show that the coming disaster was not our fault. In other words, the *will* to communicate is absent. Its place is taken by the will to mystify. Does that sound improbable? It happens every day. It happens all the time. There is a technique in communicating but no sort of technique will help us if the will is absent. All too often the will to explain is simply not there.

So much for the role of imagination, for the will to put the message over. Come now to the creation of trust. In all human relationships trust is a vital factor. For success in negotiation, it is vitally important that people will believe what you say and assume that any promise you make will be kept. But it is no good saying 'Trust me. Rely on my word.' Only politicians say that. Among businessmen trust is not given. It has to be earned. After years in the trade you may gain a reputation for being reliable and honest. People will have found that you mean what you say. It takes time to establish such a reputation. Remember, however, that you can establish yourself as a friend and neighbour before you have done any business at all. Take, for example, the ritual that surrounds our visit to the village shop. There are people who rush in and say 'A kilo of tomatoes, please.' But that is mere bad manners. The right method is to begin, 'Good morning, Mr Whatever [or George, or Sally, as the case may be]. Nice weather we are having. How are you keeping? [etc.]' You start a conversation and end up with an inquiry about tomatoes. Where the matter is of greater importance – the hiring of a truck or a senior executive, say – the approach may be more leisurely still. Why? Because you aim to be friends before the serious discussion starts. Where the matter is one of some delicacy you will spread your visits over a number of weeks. When the bargaining begins you will not be a complete stranger but someone who is known by name, a neighbour, a man who may be thought trustworthy. Now, in creating a good relationship between one firm and another, between the company and the government, between management and personnel, we have to realize that it is going to take time. The contract that we are anxious to obtain must be the reward for the good work we have done in the past.

The industrial dispute we aim to prevent is one that would take place in five or ten years' time. To prevent it, we begin talking now – not about wage differentials but about other things, horses, fishing, music or football. We have first to establish that we (the managers) are men with names, personalities, interests and, possibly, weaknesses. We are not 'they', the nameless representatives of capital, but Tom, Dick and Harry. We have next to show that the men on the shop floor are not mere personnel but are characters known to us by name and personality. They are Bill, Sam and Bob, one of them a charge hand, another a shop steward and a third (possibly) a communist. It should be possible to create a man-to-man relationship, but it will take time and effort. When you are known as a man among men you can set out to prove that you are also a man to be trusted. When you promise to be there at eight you are there at eight. When you promise to keep quiet about something, you keep quiet about it. You prove over the years that what you say is the truth, that what you promise you will do. Then, at long last, a crisis comes and you realize that an industrial dispute is possible. Knowing the men as you do, you hear of the trouble long before it starts. The probable result is that it never starts at all. You are there first and you are a man they will believe. It may seem, and it is, a laborious process, but there is no other way. The dispute that begins today is the result of what someone failed to do ten years ago. The mischief is when the company is sold, the board replaced, the managers changed and the whole process put back to the starting point. This happens too often and is the cause of much that goes wrong. There has been no time to establish a relationship of mutual trust.

We have also to consider the relationship between an industrial organization and its suppliers, its rivals, its shareholders, customers, bankers, government and public. The principles that govern policy in each case may be the same but the message in each instance is likely to be different, not because our ways are devious but because different people have different interests. Shareholders want to see the balance sheet, customers want to hear of any new product, government may be interested in export plans and the public mostly concerned about pollution and perhaps profits. So the sorts of information that are to be supplied may be varied indeed. As against that, the underlying purpose must always be the same; to create a reputation for honesty, competence, public spirit and courtesy. We know, however, that such a reputation is not based upon what we say but upon what we do. Realizing this, some businessmen resolve to say little, pointing silently at their past achievement. This is, however, a serious mistake, for our past good deeds do not, of necessity, speak for themselves. If we are silent, other people will be voluble and perhaps at our expense. To talk and do nothing will give us, admittedly, a bad reputation, but to do all we should and say nothing about it may end at best with our having no reputation at all. So our task is to explain as well as to act, and we will do well to remember that the explanations should be as good as the policy.

Suppose we are now ready to convey a message, describe a situation, explain a new development. We must decide at the outset to keep it brief. Too much information is as bad as too little and has, in fact, the same effect – that is, probably, none. But how is the message to be phrased? In other words, what precisely are we trying to do? We have ceased (let us hope) to relieve our minds of what we feel or think. We shall speak with a purpose to a public we have clearly in mind. What shall we say in order to persuade these particular people to do something or perhaps to refrain from doing something? It does not matter how the message sounds to us. How will it sound to them? Begin with the content of the message. What, briefly, do you want to say? Remember that the commonest cause of disaster, in all human affairs, is an initial failure to decide what you are trying to do. Suppose there are two projects, A and B. You will often find that one of them, project B, has attracted a thick file of untidy correspondence, with minutes, reports, committee recommendations and specialists' advice. Project A, achieving more, has attracted less paper, the file being thin, clean and neat. Go back to enclosure 1A on File A and you will find that the policy was well defined from the outset. Go back to enclosure 1A on File B and you will find that the object in view has never been properly defined. On that shaky foundation there has been built up a mountain of correspondence and little real achievement. Go wrong at the beginning and nothing will afterwards go right.

The basic question is always 'What are we trying to do – and why?' It is told of Peter Drucker that he was called in as consultant by a firm that manufactured glass bottles. At his first meeting with the board he asked them, 'In what business are you engaged?' Slightly annoyed (for he should, after all, have read the literature they had given him), the President replied, 'We are in the business of manufacturing glass bottles.' To this Drucker is said to have replied, 'No you are not. You are in the packaging business.' The directors were suddenly made to see a great truth. Beer must be packaged but not, of necessity, in glass. In two short sentences Drucker had made the directors think, perhaps (who knows?) for the first time. Apply the same question to a school. If we ask the teachers, 'What are you doing and why?' we shall be surprised at the variety of answers we receive. We may not know what the right answer should be but we shall discover, in minutes, why so little is being achieved. The object in view has never been defined. At the present time Britain is fighting a minor civil war in Northern Ireland, a confused conflict in which politicians, soldiers, police and informers are all more or less involved. Will they suceed? How can they? Succeed in what? Nobody has ever made a clear definition of a feasible task. Success is therefore impossible and will remain so until those responsible go back to the beginning, ask the right questions and give the right answers. All current operations are a waste of time. Nor are commercial or industrial projects any different. We must do our thinking first. What is our aim, our object; what, exactly, are we trying to do?

Let us assume that we have a message to put over and have decided exactly what it is; there are still some rules to observe. First of all, we must refrain from putting it over too often. Internally we should avoid issuing new notices every day, new rules every week, a plan for reorganization every month and a change of policy every year. Too much communication is as harmful as too little. Tell people what they need to know but do not swamp them with information and exhortation. Second, remember that communication is a two-way process. You must test the reaction and you must sense when there is a feeling of resentment on the factory floor. It is a sign of failure when a deputation comes to complain about something. You should have known sooner about the complaint and taken action to remedy or explain it. The good manager can smell unrest just as the good sea captain can sense panic or mutiny. Third, we should never forget that it is often possible to distract attention from a sore subject, giving people something else to think and talk about. When sufficiently excited about something like a football match or a band performance, we can forget about a lot of discomfort. The player, coming off the field, finds that he has a bruise on the shin – he did not notice the kick that made the bruise in the first place. A part of the art of management lies in the ability to distract attention. That is how to reconcile people to a necessary inconvenience, by finding a partial remedy before people have even expressed their grievance.

Externally, the task is more complex. There will be a reduced dividend this year and a larger transfer of funds to reserve. The shareholders will want to know why. Some employees have become redundant, the result of automation. The explanation must be candid and convincing, and the treatment of those displaced must be fair and must be seen to be fair. There is to be a new factory at X despite the rumours that have been current of an even bigger development at Y. Assurances must be given about the employment situation at Y and the environmental disaster impending at X. There is a public outcry about the danger of fire said to be inherent in plastic product Z. The danger is non-existent but we need to conciliate the well-meaning folk who made the complaint. With a little ingenuity we can turn the adverse publicity into an actual advertisement for the product. The ordeal by fire might even be televised. . . . Our goods are blacked by trade union W because we insist on exporting to our old business partners in Afrasia. How can we bring pressure to bear upon the officials of union W, who are thus about to cause unemployment among the members of union V? The situations multiply in which we have to explain ourselves with lucidity, honesty, conviction, eloquence, brevity and speed.

Come now to the question of style in communication. Style is, first and foremost, the imprint of character upon action. A warship comes into port at speed, swings alongside the wharf with a flourish and all with a minimum number of orders. In a matter of minutes she is secure, a gangway is down and a sentry is at the end of it. Watching the process, a knowledgeable onlooker will say, 'That will be Captain Dashing – I can recognize his style.' An announcement, a message, can and should convey a sense of character. It should not be a colourless or civil service-type pronouncement. While precise and terse, it should go beyond precision and brevity. It should be coloured by the personality of the chief executive. This personal touch can be achieved in several ways or by a combination of several methods. Here are three, to begin with. First, it should come from the man himself, not from a nameless and faceless authority, commonly described as 'they'. It should be signed by the chief executive, a man who should be known to all by sight and to some at least by daily contact. Second, it should never include long words and involved constructions. Words of one syllable are best, each word a hammer blow rather than a handful of cotton wool. Third, it should sometimes include a touch of humour, and this for two reasons. In the first place, humour makes it human rather than impersonal. In the second place, people remember a joke when they forget everything else.

The challenge to businessmen is, in essence, the future survival of business enterprise. This requires a vigorous defence of its legitimate freedoms and a mature acceptance of change in industrial policy and practice to be in step and not in conflict with the social and political environment of which it is a key element. Effective communication, in its many forms, is the one essential catalyst to meeting this challenge. Thus far it has proved to be the illusive missing link between business enterprise and both its public acceptance and understanding, between the legitimate objectives of industry and both the aspirations and expectations of those who work in it.

It would be well if we could assume, as we may tend to assume, that businessmen feel the need to communicate. The fact is, however, that they have a long tradition of reticence, a tradition however, that now seems to be changing, as we shall discover in the next chapter.

SECTION TWO

The groups that affect industry and its freedom – their key characteristics and communication needs

3. Business Leaders
4. Government
5. Stockholders and Investors
6. Workers and Their Representatives
7. Teachers and Students
8. Special Interest Groups
9. The Press

3

Business Leaders

The new breed of European managers blame its predecessors (as new breeds are apt to) for an ineffective response before the problem became a crisis. They feel industry itself should have defended the good in free enterprise more vigorously and reformed the unacceptable more purposefully. They know industry is not guilty on all counts of the charge against it, and resent management's historical inability to enter a plea in the court of public opinion.

The most successful businessmen are coming out of their shells.

They are developing a new awareness of the need for industry to communicate more effectively and with many more elements of society than ever before. There is a greater recognition of the need to communicate more effectively as a part of the day-to-day management of a company. There is also some recognition of the need to communicate more effectively to influence the public and political climate in which business must operate. In all respects business leaders sense the consequences of past failures.

These are among the conclusions to be drawn from some fifty personal interviews and formal opinion research conducted exclusively for this book among a representative sample of more than four hundred chief executives in the four major industrial nations of Europe – Germany, France, Britain and Italy.

THE SURVEY

The opinion survey was conducted by Landell Mills Associates of London in co-operation with Management Centre Europe, Brussels. It investigated company policy and practice in communicating with some twenty internal and external 'publics'. We wanted to find out what companies are doing at the moment and what the chief executive feels industry should be doing to state its case and explain its activities and achievements.

The gap between what companies do at the moment and what chief executives feel industry should be doing is extraordinarily wide. So too is the amount of time that chief executives currently spend and think they will (or should) spend personally on communicating with various groups in the future.

Of the chief executives questioned, 80 per cent think that the amount of information communicated by companies *will* increase over the next five years and 89 per cent think it *should* (27 per cent think it will 'increase *greatly*' and 40 per cent think it should). Most of those questioned spend much less than 20 per cent of their time on company communications, the most frequently mentioned figures being 'about 5 per cent' and 'about 10 per cent'. However, 60 per cent think this level will increase over the next five years (10 per cent saying it will 'increase greatly') and 76 per cent say they think it *should* increase (20 per cent saying it should 'increase greatly'). Most think the amount of time that chief executives *should* spend personally on communicating with various internal and external groups is between 15 and 25 per cent.

But the survey, a summary of whose findings is given later in this chapter, betrayed a short-sightedness among chief executives in some important respects. For example, it revealed that: 'Relations with the non-business community are much less widely felt to be important objectives . . . the further from the factory gate a public is, the less important it is thought to be . . . [and] the less frequently they are addressed.'

In one sense this indicates a sensible allocation of priorities. Obviously a company's own workers and business associates should be its most important 'publics', and this is what our survey indicates. But, as we shall discover in later chapters, the low priority industry has given, and in some cases continues to give, to those 'further from the factory gate' has fostered many of the problems facing industry today.

Students and teachers fall into this category. Only one company in four claims to communicate with these 'at least once a year'. Yet they are, on the one hand, the workers and managers of tomorrow and, on the other, the people who shape their ideals and expectations. Our survey indicates that the need to do more in this area is recognized to some extent – but will it be enough and will it be in time? The same is true for members of parliamentary assemblies, international, political and economic agencies and environmental and consumer organizations. Many companies can claim that their production processes and products do not bring them into conflict with environmental and consumer protection groups. But virtually none, whatever their size or industry, can claim to be unaffected by the attitudes and actions of government.

The survey revealed surprisingly few differences between the views of chief executives in the four countries in which it was conducted. One difference, however, was the way in which they responded to the survey itself. German chief executives returned the survey questionnaire promptly, often with a brief but polite covering letter. Some of the French and most of the Italian chief executives took a long time to return the questionnaires – and fewer Italians than any other nationality responded at all. British respondents, however, divided into two groups – those who returned the questionnaires promptly, and several dozen who wrote at some length to explain that they were far too busy to respond. The chief executive of one British company kindly wrote a detailed three-page letter explaining why he did not have the time to complete our four-page questionnaire.

It was clear from the survey that the larger companies communicate more information, more frequently, and to more people than do smaller ones. This, perhaps, was to be expected. The amount of time that chief executives spend personally, however, on communicating bears no relation at all to company size. One of the key factors here seems to be age. Although this point was not covered by the research survey, the interviews we conducted (among other factors) lead us to conclude that the younger chief executives tend to spend much more time communicating than their older colleagues. Indeed, there is evidence to endorse the concept of a new breed of executive emerging in the upper reaches of management and in the board rooms of European industry. Most of the business leaders we interviewed had a clear and consistent perception of this new breed.

He (and increasingly she) has risen through the industrial ranks, often beginning a career outside management. He has a predominantly postwar education. He has little or no capital, and what money he has managed to accumulate is seldom invested in company stock (except when he has access to a company stock-option plan). He is widely travelled and much more international in outlook than the man he has replaced. He is more sensitive and responsive than his predecessor to social and political pressures, in addition to the traditional competitiveness of industrial enterprise. He is more professional.

He is no longer a rarity in top management. Nor is he commonplace. But there are many more like him in middle management waiting to move up.

Much of this new breed sees itself as the phoenix rising from the ashes of an autocratic past, facing problems and pressures that have been created in part by a stubborn and feudal management of yester-year. Industry now faces intolerable pressures from over-government, too much legislation and regulation, disgruntled workers and disappointed stockholders, persistent environmental and consumer protection groups and a hostile public climate. The new breed of managers blames its predecessors (as new breeds are apt to) for an ineffective response before the problem became a crisis. They feel industry itself should have defended the good in free enterprise more vigorously and reformed the unacceptable more purposefully. They know industry is not guilty on all counts of the charge against it, and resent management's historical inability to enter a plea in the court of public opinion.

THE MANAGERS' OWN VIEWS

According to Bernt J. Grondahl, managing director of the Norwegian America Line,

> the new breed of European manager is in part a reflection of industry's voluntary response in some countries to industrial democracy; and he is also beginning to drag the less responsive elements of industry into twentieth century Europe. His most prominent characteristics are his international outlook, his sensitivity to the legitimate aspirations of others, and his willingness and ability to communicate effectively. He still accepts the historical challenge to management of allocating resources wisely to produce goods and services that will generate a profit to ensure the future survival of his business. But he also accepts that his task is bound up with a much wider responsibility to his employees and society as a whole.

Jacques Maisonrouge, chairman of IBM World Trade Corporation and president of IBM Europe, notes a big difference in the qualities required of a senior manager in Europe today compared with one or two decades ago. 'The successful manager in Europe today has to operate more on the basis of consensus than autocracy,' says Maisonrouge:

> He must ask himself 'if there were to be an election in the company for

my present position, would I retain the job?' If he is not certain the answer would be 'yes', he must at least discover why. It may be that for sound business reasons he has had to take some very unpopular decisions – but has he done all he could or should to explain why those decisions were necessary? Management by acceptance, which is the practical reality of running a business in most of Europe today, requires skills in communication and persuasion that the autocratic entrepreneur rarely possesses. The new breed of manager does possess these skills. His origins, outlook and expectations are different.

Maisonrouge also sees this concept of 'management by acceptance' in a much wider context than just within the company.

The same principles apply to a company's relationship with other essential elements of society – be it government, the local community in which a company has a factory, or the schools and universities that will provide industry with the employees of tomorrow. In every case, the role of industry, its needs and limitations, must be understood. Understanding results from effective communication of relevant information. Most management failures result from or are accentuated by a failure to communicate somewhere along the line. Recognition of this need to communicate ought to be written into the job specification of every chief executive and senior manager.

Some of the new concepts in business and man management are especially prevalent in northern Europe – most notably in Germany, Austria, the Netherlands and the Scandinavian countries. And they are found in men like Philip Rosenthal, chairman and chief executive of Rosenthal AG, the German manufacturer of porcelain, glass and furniture.

In addition to running a successful business, Rosenthal is a member of Germany's Bundestag and a former government junior minister. He has played a leading role in his country's development of worker participation (and has contributed a case-study on the subject in section four of this book – see Chapter 17). 'The future of free enterprise in Europe lies squarely in the Continent's acceptance of industrial democracy – workers participating in the "saying" [i.e. co-determination] and the "having" [i.e. capital sharing],' Rosenthal contends:

Certainly this sometimes makes management more difficult, sometimes a little slower, but these disadvantages are nothing to the avoidance of confrontation between property and labour which helps neither. We can see where confrontation leads to, both economically and politically, in several European countries. If Germany has weathered the international crisis better, it is in the first place because workers here are more a part of their company. As in any other field, one only understands and supports organizations in which one participates. This means, of course, that communication becomes more important. Participation only works when the participating worker is informed.

Rosenthal also believes that the same qualities required of management in an industrial democracy spill over into other areas of management responsibility:

> The new breed of manager, who has the sensitivity and personal awareness required to operate a company well in a participative environment, is also concerned about the morality of his company – the quality and usefulness of its products, the effects of its manufacturing processes and products on the environment, the quality of its contribution to the community in which it operates. This is an inevitable characteristic in a manager who is a sensitive and intelligent receiver as well as transmitter of ideas and information. The process of communication in this context is not only healthy for the individual company; but also for the contribution and reputation of industry as a whole.

Many managers, however, are more cautious than Philip Rosenthal. They note that, while the new breed of manager is beyond the 'prototype' phase, 'production' is unlikely to satisfy the 'demand' for his skills for some time. For many countries, too, especially in southern Europe, worker participation and industrial democracy remain the riddle within the enigma. This is certainly true also of American industry, including much of it that operates in Europe.

While there are probably far too many intellectuals running businesses in Europe, there are far too few in the U.S.A. American businessmen tend to be more numerate than literate, while the reverse tends to be true of the average European businessman. The American businessman is oriented much more towards the short-term financial success of his company than his European counterpart whose decisions are often affected by longer-term considerations. The American businessman is more inclined than his European contemporary to regard his workers as a resource that can be acquired or dispensed with at short notice according to the levels required to fill the order book.

The American businessman will say he is operating in a time-frame in which the governing factors are either known or predictable, while the European will spend much more time considering the impact of decisions taken today on the social and economic performance of his company tomorrow – tomorrow being perhaps several years hence. This relative lack of concern for the immediate future, except when it is a question of survival, is reflected in the businessman's personal habits, too. Lunching with an American executive, you will be talking business before the soup arrives, whereas with the European you may be getting round to it over coffee. The European businessman is much more willing than his American counterpart to sacrifice today's profits for tomorrow's prosperity.

So long as a company is operating only in one or the other continent, life may be relatively simple. The problem comes when a company operates on both sides of the Atlantic and tries to operate with a single philosophy. Playing the game in Europe by American rules leads inevitably to frustration and friction. Playing the game in America by European rules can be disastrous.

The American business executive's fundamental adaptability to business opportunity is clearly his greatest strength. After all, American business was able to exploit the commercial opportunities of the European dream and operate across national borders more readily than its more cautious and tradition-bound European counterparts. Additionally, European businessmen can hardly believe, let alone use to full effect, the commercial and competitive freedom available to them in the American market. Against this, however, one must set the European's ability to respond more subtly to social change and political pressure, relying on a political sophistication that the average American businessman may often lack.

The American has a certain directness, born out of his haste for action, compared with the European businessman who may have considerably more patience and tact. The rightness or relevance of either approach will depend very much on the individual problem or opportunity, of course, and the trick is to use either approach according to the circumstances, or manage somehow to combine the two.

Europeans and Americans have learnt much from each other in postwar Europe. European executives have learnt about production and marketing techniques from more adventurous American colleagues or rivals. Americans have learnt, or are learning, the merits of greater subtlety. But here we seem to have reached the end of a chapter. Within the context of its own now-unique environment, European industry has probably learnt all it will from once technically superior American business methods. At the same time the current level of American business investment in Europe probably far exceeds the needs of United States foreign and economic policy. Coupled with this, the attractiveness of Europe from a purely economic standpoint has been overtaken and reversed by events. Now, relatively unstable currencies, not to mention national political environments, make 'doing business at home in the USA' a much more attractive alternative from a pragmatic and short-term standpoint.

'The fact is that the rules are changing much faster for management in Europe than in America,' says Michel Bergerac, chairman and president of Revlon Inc. and a former president of ITT Europe.

Europe is an environment that many Americans find increasingly difficult to accept and work with. Indeed, Europe is now so 'foreign' to many American managers that they are apt to see alien and radical ghosts under the European industrial bed that are often not there. Such hallucinations frequently lead to needless friction.

The communication demands on management in America are much different to those in Europe, too. Corporate communication is more important in America in one respect – it is expected. What makes it easier, however, it that the priorities and issues are more clearly defined. American industry is governed much more by the legislative process. A company's communication with various groups (government, stockholders, minorities, and so forth) is conditioned by legal responsibilities. In Europe, perceived responsibility and legal requirement overlap much less precisely. The European will say he is operating in a more subtle environment. With equal justification, the American will say it is more vague.

America is a more challenging environment than Europe in a commercial and competitive sense, but Europe presents many more challenges in social and man management areas [Bergerac concludes]. Success or failure in this context rests on an understanding of the issues, and an ability to communicate well – the ability to speak up as well as listen.

A related comment comes from Dr John Nicholls, director of the European Management Forum:

The political and social drift of Europe over the past decade or so has pushed industrial enterprise into a defensive position, pilloried by public opinion and hounded by restrictive legislation. Indeed, many would say the foundations of its competitiveness in world markets may be threatened. Management in Europe has a choice, however. It can allow the drift to continue in any direction that politics and public opinion will take it or it can attempt to influence that drift. If it decides on the latter course, it decides to become a more active advocate, a more purposeful communicator, and a constructive participant in the public debate on the future of free enterprise.

THE NEED TO COMMUNICATE

Indeed, the need for industry to take this 'latter course' is among the demands on European industry that are being discussed more and more frequently in the corridors of industrial power. For example, at the 1977 European Management Forum ('management symposium') at Davos, Switzerland, it was one of the more frequent coffee-break and cocktail discussion points, and emerged several times during ten days of formal presentations and workshop debates. The symposium is probably the most prestigious annual event for top management in Europe and now attracts more than 600 business leaders from Europe and the rest of the world. The theme of the 1977 symposium was 'Competing Successfully in a World of Social and Structural Change'. The need for industry to communicate its problems and achievements in this context was perhaps put most succinctly in a debate on 'Freedom and Prosperity through Competitive Free Enterprise' by Sir Keith Joseph, Bt, MP, director of the Centre for Policy Studies, London: 'Industry simply has not put its case. It has allowed itself to be shouted down by the enemies of free enterprise and has hardly entered the debate at all. It is a most urgent problem.'

Not only did our European survey support the need for increased communication skills at the chief executive level; but it has been 'one of the biggest growth areas in management education during the past couple of years', according to Clement Livingstone, managing director of Management Centre Europe. MCE is the European arm of the American Management Associations and claims to be Europe's largest management development and information organization. 'Courses that help the senior manager cope with public speaking and probing question-and-answer situations (on the shop floor, with the media or pressure groups) have become increasingly important in our curriculum.' But Livingstone takes this development a stage further and links it with the new breed of European manager:

> The industrial environment of Europe today has certainly created a need for management to communicate; but what distinguishes the new breed of manager from his predecessor is that he actually *wants* to communicate. Not only does he know that his success as a manager, and the success of his business, depends upon it; he actively enjoys the

process of communication. He has also developed a number of other skills related to the art of communication, psychological skills that help him understand the diversity of individuals and groups with which he must deal, negotiate and bargain. This is especially true in the area of non-verbal communication.

'Such managers are in increasing demand, and no longer just in Europe. They are highly prized individuals among recruitment consultants and head-hunters.' Livingstone says:

> European industry is already moving into America in a big way. It will take advantage of the greater entrepreneurial freedom there; but it may also be the trojan horse of new concepts in business and man management. I would not exclude the possibility of some elements of European industrial democracy crossing the Atlantic. It may well prove the basis for a new brain-drain of European managers going to America in five-to-ten years.

THE ROLE OF COMPANY COMMUNICATION – THE OPINIONS OF CHIEF EXECUTIVES

To ascertain the opinions of chief executives on various aspects of company communication policy and practice we commissioned more extensive attitude research on the subject than has ever been undertaken in Europe before. The research was conducted by Landell Mills Associates* in co-operation with Management Centre Europe. We wanted to determine the views of company chief executive officers in Europe's four major industrial nations on some clearly defined aspects of current company communication policy and practice, and on an optimum future policy for industry as a whole. We wanted to know which groups are, and should in future be regarded as, important, what information is, and should be, communicated, and how much of the chief executive's time is, and should be, spent on the development and implementation of communication policy. For the purpose of the survey we excluded communication directly aimed at sales promotion. For validity, and to enable us to make comparisons between countries, size of company and so forth, we needed to have the views of a large number of chief executives.

Two separate four-page questionnaires, one primarily designed to identify current practice and the other to determine the chief executives' views on an optimum future policy, were sent to two matched samples of

---

* The market research activities of Landell Mills Associates have since been merged into Research Services Ltd.

1,000 chief executives in Germany, France, Britain and Italy. More than 400 responded, a little more than 200 on each questionnaire, the respondents to both being perfectly matched in terms of country of origin, company size and type of industry. Analysis of the returned questionnaires was supplemented by telephone interviews with several of the respondents whose replies called for more detailed examination.

The research was designed by Nick Winkfield of Landell Mills Associates who also analysed the returned questionnaires and prepared the following notes summarizing his findings.

Benefits of Company Communication

The main benefits that chief executives expect to derive from communication programmes are improved relations within the company and a better-quality executive recruitment (see Table 1). However, long-term (not short-term) sales increases are often seen as a benefit as is support from financial institutions. Relations with the non-business community are much less widely felt to be important objectives.

Table 1

Benefit	Proportion of chief executives thinking each benefit important: to their own company	to companies in general
	%	%
Better executive morale	86	93
Long-term sales increases	78	77
Better labour relations in general	76	80
Better quality of executive recruitment	70	86
Greater support from financial institutions	63	77
Employee/union support on specific issues	56	64
Immediate sales increases	43	33
Better understanding among special interest groups	44	67
Better local community relations	40	60
General public support and understanding of company objectives	39	58
Government support on specific issues	35	50
Better government relations in general	24	43

More chief executives believe that companies in general derive a wide range of benefits from company communications than do their own particular companies, especially where relations with the non-business community are concerned. (Indeed, the further from the factory gate a public is, the less important it is thought to be.)

Differences between Current Practice and The Ideal Company Policy

The gap between current practice and what is desirable is well illustrated by chief executives' views about whether information should be given on an on-going basis or restricted to specific *ad hoc* occasions: 39 per cent currently have on-going programmes, as opposed to communicating *ad hoc*, but 58 per cent think that the on-going approach would benefit companies in general.

It is interesting that the UK chief executives favour on-going programmes much more than the French and Italians do, and that the Germans, who are typical in their views about what would benefit companies in general, hardly ever seem to run on-going programmes in practice (less than 10 per cent of our sample in Germany claimed to do so).

It is possible that the chief executives think their own companies are different from others, and need less PR and communication. (Indeed, some differences such as company size may well affect the extent of the communication needed.) It is perhaps not surprising that more large than small companies consider relations with non-business groups to be important, and believe in on-going communication projects. But this does not explain more than a part of the wide gap between 'one's own company' and 'companies in general': even in the companies with 500 or more employees the difference is marked. None of the other factors that might have influenced replies in this way, such as industrial sector, or national/foreign ownership, in fact do so to any great extent.

It seems, therefore, that there is a real gap between current practice and the ideal.

Chief executives told us: 'Our product is the only PR we need,' 'We don't have much to do with consumer groups,' and 'We don't need to rely on the local community, unlike Company X,' 'My main concern is with my customers and the bank, though I can quite see that industry as a whole has an environmental problem to solve,' and even 'The Government can't really affect our sales' (the last from a company whose main market is the British shipbuilding industry!). On the other hand, many companies may feel that they would benefit from increased PR and communication activity but have not yet got around to it. Two typical quotations were: 'I think we would benefit from wider communications, but it is low on my priority list,' and 'So far our PR has been limited, but I think this will have to change in the future.' These may well have contributed to the gap between current practice and the ideal.

Table 2

Publics with whom companies do and should communicate regularly	Currently	Ideally
	%	%
Business and industrial leaders		
Trade customers	59	78
Suppliers	45	62
Business and trade organizations	61	75
Senior executives in other companies	43	35
Government		
MPs, delegates	18	42
Government officials	43	43
International political and economic agencies	17	39
Financial publics		
Banks	89	92
Institutional investors	28	70
Private stockholders	58	92
Employees and their respresentatives		
Top management	92	97
Middle management	91	96
Other employees	81	92
Trade union leaders	35	59
Educators and students		
Educators	25	40
Students	26	42
Special interest groups		
Local community leaders	33	57
Consumer organizations	15	56
Environmental organizations	18	46
The general public	37	65

The implication to be drawn from this is that the extent of company communications will increase in the future. Indeed, the chief executives who took part in the survey endorse this forecast: 80 per cent think the amount of information released will increase during the next five years, and no less than 89 per cent think it should (27 per cent and 40 per cent respectively think it will or should increase *greatly.*) Practically nobody thinks the amount of information given will actually decrease.

Chief executives in all four countries share this view, although the British and French express it rather more strongly than the Germans and Italians. As we would anticipate, those in the large companies are rather more likely than others to expect increases.

In all but two of the categories in Table 2 it is clear that current practice falls short of the ideal. It also seems that, apart from the banks, the further people are from the factory gate the less frequently they are addressed.

The Chief Executive's Personal Involvement

Personal involvement by chief executives in company communications is also expected to increase, if the differences between current practice and the 'ideal' are taken as a guide. Most of those included in the survey currently spend less than 20 per cent of their time on these activities, and by far the most frequently mentioned figures are 'about 5 per cent' and 'about 10 per cent'. But the 'ideal' amount of time is rather less widely thought to be 5 per cent, and more often 15, 20 or 25 per cent.

It is interesting that 12 per cent of the survey sample estimate that they currently spend more than 40 per cent of their time on company communications; but that only 6 per cent think that so much time is ideal. This suggests that a limit will be reached in the increasing involvement of chief executives in communications. But for the 74 per cent of them who devote less than 20 per cent of their time to these activities, the limit still seems a long way ahead.

Which publics, then, require so much personal attention from chief executives? In the survey they were asked to name their three key publics, and eight emerged as important (Table 3). These figures mask relatively few differences of emphasis between the four countries. However, the Italian chief executives are very seldom personally concerned with environmental organizations, either currently or in their assessment of the ideal; and the French, who currently spend more of their time with employees other than management, would ideally devote much less time to them than to trade customers, banks or environmental organizations.

Table 3

Key publics to companies	Currently	Ideally
	%	%
Trade customers	31	29
Employees, other than management	28	20
Environmental organizations	21	34
Banks	22	23
Consumer organizations	15	15
Middle management	10	14
Private stockholders	11	14
Government officials	9	11

The chief executives, other than in Italy, place much greater personal emphasis on environmental and consumer organizations than their total company activities would suggest. Asked how often companies, as opposed to the chief executives personally, do and should give information to various publics, both of these were accorded a low priority, and company management rises to the top of the list.

What to Communicate

The subject matter of corporate communications, both in practice and in the ideal situation, depends upon the public to be addressed. The information most often given to the financial community is about financial performance and company prospects, followed by new capital investments. The commercial publics (customers, suppliers, business organizations) are told most often about product and commercial developments, followed by major achievements in technology, company prospects and new capital investments (in that order). Government and official bodies are told most about company prospects, then technological achievements and labour relations. Finally, the environmental and consumer organizations are most often informed about technological and product matters, with company prospects and new capital investments given a lower priority. All of this is what one might expect.

However, with very few exceptions, more information is thought desirable than is at present given to these publics, particularly about achievements in technology and company prospects. On these two subjects, 20–25 per cent more chief executives think companies would benefit by giving information than actually do.

Apart from such factual matters, companies often wish to improve their image in less tangible ways. The concepts most often featured in company communication programmes are: product quality (84 per cent), concern for the consumer (76 per cent), concern for employees (75 per cent), and strength of management (71 per cent).

These concepts are also thought in general to benefit the images of companies; but so are certain other concepts, perhaps related more to the government and official communities than to business or the public, which do not currently enjoy the same degree of exposure: financial strength, contribution to the economy, export performance and the provision of local employment all seem to deserve more attention than they receive. However, these are achievements that could not in fact be claimed by companies in general in a time of recession, however valuable they might be to the development of a company image. Hence, perhaps, the marked difference between current practice and the ideal at the present time.

Table 4 illustrates these points and details the role and value of various concepts in company communication programmes, as seen by the chief executive.

Table 4

Concepts in company communication programmes	Featured by respondent company	Benefits the image of companies in general
	%	%
Quality of products	84	91
Concern for the consumer	76	83
Concern for employees	75	82
Strong management	71	80
Range of company activities	69	66
Financial strength	66	80
Export performance	62	78
Company growth rate	61	66
R & D effort	60	68
Provision of local employment	52	71
Contribution to the economy	52	77
Concern for the environment	51	65
Social and cultural community programmes	21	30

How to Communicate

The most important single method of communicating company information is through the press; 61 per cent of the companies represented in the sample maintain press relations, and 81 per cent think it important for companies in general to do so.

Annual reports are thought to be very nearly as important, followed by other forms of direct mail. Employee newspapers and media advertising are each used by 42 per cent, although over 60 per cent think them important for companies in general.

Information Sources for Communication Planning and Communication Training

The most important source of information used in planning company communications is comment from the trade, employees and trade unions. However, over half of the chief executives claim that market and opinion research play an important part, and three-quarters think that they *should* play an important part. The sources of information thought to be important in planning company communications are shown in Table 5.

Table 5

Sources of information used in planning company communications	Current practice	Important for companies in general
	%	%
Press or TV comment	46	79
Trade comment	68	85
Employee and trade union comment	67	78
Government/official comment	44	55
Market/opinion research	54	75

The French are rather more inclined, and the Italians less inclined, than others, to rely on press or TV comment. The reliance on market or opinion research in planning company communications is heaviest in France, followed by Germany, with the United Kingdom and Italy lagging somewhat behind.

The use of market research is one indicator of the extent to which company communication programmes have been formalized and subjected to professional treatment. The use of training in the PR communication area is perhaps an even more direct indicator, and there is indeed a strong correlation between the 'use of research' statistics and the figures in Table 6. Once again, the gap between current practice and the ideal is wide, and the frequency most widely given moves from 'never' to 'every second or third year'.

A very similar picture emerges regarding the training of non-specialist managers in communication techniques.

Table 6

Frequency of formal training of PR/communication specialists	Current practice	Ideal for companies in general
	%	%
At least once a year	22	36
Every second or third year	20	43
At longer intervals	12	18
Never	46	3

4

Government

Industry has much to learn in its dealings with government and the process of legislation. Failure to do so in the past has led to unnecessarily punitive legislation and a dangerous shift in government and public attitudes to industrial enterprise. Today's circumstances call for intelligent 'preaction', open involvement in the process of government, strong advocacy of industry's viewpoint, a lot more goodwill and self-regulation.

The role of government in shaping the policies and performance of business enterprise is a growing concern for management around the world. It is perhaps especially true of Europe, where government plays a more direct role than virtually anywhere outside the Iron Curtain. Indeed, many chief executives in Europe see the increasing involvement of government, growing out of social and environmental pressures and the perceived needs of national economies, as the single most challenging problem for the future.

At a series of seminars for chief executives and their immediate subordinates, sponsored by Management Centre Europe in 1975 and 1976, an overwhelming majority of participants agreed that government encroachment on their freedom of action was the priority problem for business today. They put this slightly ahead of the constraining influences of organized labour resulting from the trend towards worker participation.

Seminar participants also felt that businessmen had sat around far too long waiting for legislation to catch up with them, and had not begun to protest until it was too late. The solution, most felt, was to get together more with government leaders and to educate them in the needs of business.

A somewhat similar conclusion can be drawn from our more extensive research among European chief executives; but the sample of more than 400 whose opinions we surveyed drew a clear distinction between government officials and elected members of parliamentary assemblies. They felt that the level of information currently given to government officials was adequate. Much less information, however, is currently given to elected members of parliament: a disturbingly low 18 per cent of those chief executives surveyed said their companies currently communicate regularly with this group. More than twice as many said they thought industry should do so, but even this seems inadequate in relation to the size of the problem perceived.

However, assuming a willingness to communicate with government, where does the businessman start to determine the levels at which the problem should be tackled?

WHERE THE POWER LIES

There are, to begin with, three distinct areas to consider in the relationship of an industrial company with government:

1. the marketing effort – a company's relationship with government as a customer, and as a developer of regulation that affects the marketing effort both at home and abroad;

2. the legislative process – a company's effect on the thinking and action of government in a broad area of legislation covering personnel policy; the parameters of prices, wages and dividends; environmental, consumer and other social considerations;

3. the acceptance of industrial enterprise – a company's effect on government thinking and legislative ambitions in terms of encouraging free enterprise or so-called 'public ownership' of specific segments of industry.

There are, in the second place, four levels of government that need be of concern to business in Europe – local, regional, national and international. At each level there is a political and executive branch. The importance of each level will vary from company to company, depending largely upon size and industry sector. It will also vary from country to country because of the structure and political direction of government itself. The reorganization of postwar Germany, for example, laid great emphasis on regional government under the umbrella of a central federal government in Bonn, while most other European countries have very strong central governments with limited powers delegated to regional authorities.

It is interesting to note in this context, however, that more and more political power in European nations is now being devolved to regional authorities. Some of these have their own parliamentary assemblies. The trend is clear in Britain, where increased autonomy will clearly be passed to Scotland and Wales when the London Parliament can agree on a political formula for it. There is growing pressure also for greater delegation of power to the regions in a number of other countries, notably in Belgium, France and Spain.

At the international level, organizations like the OECD and those attached to the United Nations have considerable moral influence but no real power. The European Economic Community (or, simply, the European Community, as it now prefers to be called) is the only international government entity with any effective power in Europe. The European Community has three interrelated groups in its power structure:

1. The European Parliament. At the moment this consists of delegates sent from the national parliamentary assemblies of member states. Until the early 1970s, when it was empowered to exercise some authority over Community budgets, its primary role was to serve as a forum for public debate. In 1978, for the first time, the European Parliament will become an elected assembly. There are strong hopes that its significance and influence will increase as a result.

2. The European Commission. This is both the engine-room of the European Community and its executive branch. It is the generator of ideas and legislative proposals and the executor of approved policies and directives. It has a staff of some 7,000 international civil servants recruited from all the member states, and has to deal with some 400 Brussels-based pressure groups from trades unions to business associations.

3. The Council of Ministers. This is where the real power lies at the moment, for it is the Council that decides policy. It consists of cabinet ministers from the national governments of each state. It meets frequently to review, modify, approve or reject proposals from the Commission.

The nine European nations that comprise today's European Community represent one-seventh of the geographical area of the United States; its GNP is two-thirds of, and its population exceeds, that of the United States. Progress of the European Community towards the original dream, articulated in 1946 by Winston Churchill, of a United States of Europe has lost momentum in recent years. This has been due in part to a lack of real political leadership at the European level, but still more to the economic recession of the mid-1970s. This created a massive shift in political priorities in the member states and caused a revival of policies based on national self-interest. This unhappy turn of events came just at the point when the European Community had completed most of its easier tasks (creation of a viable customs union, a common agricultural policy (CAP), the free movement of labour within the Community and a harmonization of many aspects of the relationship between Community member states and the rest of the world). It was beginning to develop policies that would really limit national sovereignty (like economic unity, a Euro-currency and political integration). This is not to deny, however, that progress has been made towards European integration. Nor should we forget how long it took an entirely new nation like the United States to achieve integration worthy of the name. After all, America's Civil War over the individual rights of member states came some seventy years after it gained independence.

In the same way, the direction of European Community policy has been on an inevitable collision course with national chauvinism and it has proved, if proof were needed, that political power in Europe is still firmly vested in the national governments.

Despite pressure for greater delegation of power to the regions, and despite the hopes of and progress towards economic and political union at the European level, national governments are supreme and will so remain for some years to come. National government in Europe is a possible ally in foreign trade, increasingly the owner of industrial enterprise as well as key national resources, sometimes a customer, a pretender to the role of social conscience, the collector of taxes – and, above all, the legislator and regulator of our lives, both personal and corporate.

GOVERNMENT INTERVENTION

The impact of national government on the policy, performance and behaviour of business enterprise has never been stronger than it is today, and the pace seems to be accelerating. It has been one of the most marked characteristics of the postwar era and a product of the various forms of socialism that have pervaded the politics of virtually every country in Western Europe. Those nations that did not follow this general drift through a gradual democratic process had it thrust upon them, sometimes with one rapid stroke of political upheaval (as in Greece and Portugal). Even those governments that do not call themselves socialist or social democratic, as in France, have social policies that would have been considered left of centre a decade ago. Many so-called conservative political parties in other countries, now in opposition, are promising many measures of social and industrial reform too.

Aside from legislation in such areas as worker participation and other aspects of the welfare state and social reform, the two aspects of government activity that worry businessmen most are:

1. the plethora of new legislation and the resulting expansion of government agencies to control and regulate virtually every aspect of industrial enterprise – prices and wages, dividends, product content and quality, safety and environmental protection both within and outside manufacturing locations, complex systems of taxation, etc. etc.;

2. the increasing role of government in the ownership of industrial enterprise, either directly through nationalization or indirectly through government-financed super-holding companies and state-owned financial institutions.

The first of these worries is common to most of the Western world. The problem is three-fold. First, it restricts the freedom of enterprise to the extent, some claim, that there is little practical freedom left. Second, the required expansion of government agencies enlarges the proportion of non-productive workers to quite dangerous levels. Third, and related to the second point, business enterprise itself has had to add a great number of non-productive staff to its payroll to cope with the resulting paperwork and reporting requirements. This is a particularly onerous burden upon the smaller company, but it is also a matter of increasing concern for big business as well, because that tends to be more visible and vulnerable in the event of its failure to meet the required standards and reporting demands of government.

Government has, however, a number of legitimate concerns about the performance of industry in both an economic and social context. Government recognizes, of course, though not always publicly, that its achievement is controlled very largely by the viability, stability, productivity and profitability of industrial enterprise – the power-house of any nation's economic and social performance. Government regulation of industry tends to fall into two categories, therefore: first, that which influences its social and economic performance; second, that which requires it to report on actual and potential performance so that political policies and ambitions can be built for the future. Government has a necessary interest in the effects of industrial performance on unemployment, investment in new plant and technology, exports and balance of payments, profits and taxes. Priorities will of course differ from country to country. For example, talk about a favourable export performance in Britain and the businessman is a lauded hero. In Germany the same message attracts little public enthusiasm because Germany does not have a balance of payments problem.

Government has a legitimate need for statistical data on actual and projected industrial performance upon which it can base future social and economic policy. This is a need that industry must satisfy, not without question, but certainly without too much complaint when it is justified. Few businessmen would deny all need for regulation, and few would quarrel with a great deal of existing legislation. What worries them rather is the trend, and the fact that little effort is made to reduce the burden where this is possible. In the United States, for example, two presidential task forces have looked into the question of business being over-regulated and over-surveyed, and one reportedly concluded that there were 'nearly a million reports reporting that there was nothing to report'. In a major article entitled 'Strangling in Red Tape', *International Management* cites a dozen or more examples of the over-regulation of business in Europe as well as America. The article draws on a recent study by the Conference Board, a US business-supported research organization, which concluded that the two most critical issues facing business today are declining public confidence in business and government over-regulation. Significantly, it finds both factors inextricably linked and argues that 'the increasing legislation of business operations evolves in large part from the public's demands for government control because the public distrusts business'.

The second major concern we mentioned, the increasing role of government in the ownership of business enterprise, is much more of a factor in Europe than America, of course. This has been a key characteristic and product of European postwar politics. It is the second of three types of capitalism described in a two-part article by Nicholas Davenport published in Britain's *Spectator:* 'First, the obsolete, bad old bourgeois capitalism; second, the welfare or mixed economy capitalism, under which we are now suffering; and third, the state capitalism, which is communism, into which we are now sliding if we don't take care.'

Davenport argues that the problem with welfare capitalism is that the public sector enlarges itself at the expense of the private sector, so that national resources are not used or exploited economically or efficiently. The danger is that it may end up through economic mismanagement in the third form of capitalism – communism.

In some countries, like Italy, where a third of the electorate voted communist in 1976, half of industry is already owned directly or indirectly by government. About a quarter of Britain's industry is in government hands and the percentage will undoubtedly increase as the government-financed National Enterprise Board continues to rescue some companies and simply acquire others. In France, if the socialist alliance were to win the next general election, a long list of already identified large companies will be nationalized. Indeed, in countries such as France much so-called private industry is already being financed by state-owned banks and insurance companies. These state-owned financial institutions are known in France as *'les gendarmes'* because of their role in policing and regulating the country's economy.

There is an arguable logic to state ownership of natural resources, and perhaps also of the utilities and industries of national strategic importance. What worries the businessman, however, is the insidious creeping socialism that is gradually nibbling away at industrial enterprise. It is the trend, as well as today's reality, that causes alarm.

It is clear that government attitudes towards business in both Europe and America are affected by a public mistrust of private enterprise and a fundamental belief that, left to its own devices, business would harm the general good of the community. Indeed, for this reason, the business executive has a credibility problem when expressing a business viewpoint because his ambitions are thought to be further from popular social needs than those of the teacher, journalist or politician might be.

Government attitudes to business, especially in the executive branch in much of Europe, are also strongly conditioned by the personal attitudes and prejudices of those in government service. A current concern for business in much of Europe is that school-leavers and university graduates would mostly prefer a career in government or the academic world to one in industry.

In some countries this bias is all too evident, especially among the better qualified. In Britain, for example, it is rare for an honours graduate to seek a career in industry – and those that do seldom reach the top. The Civil Service is a preferred career and always has been in that country, along with the military services and the City. Britain has a strong civil service tradition going back to the days of Empire, and certain ministries like the Treasury and Foreign Office attract more than their share of the available talent. France too has a strong civil service which has always tended to attract the nation's academic élite. Indeed, the country's whole education system is geared to identifying the brilliant at an early age so as to channel them into one of the *'grandes écoles'* where they are specially trained in the arts of public administration.

Other countries, like Germany for example, have no great civil service tradition and as a result the nation's academic talent has been more evenly shared with industry.

WHAT SHOULD INDUSTRY DO?

So what should industry do about the problem of government attitudes towards it? How can it save what is left of its diminishing freedom?

In an American Management Association paper on 'Business, Government and the Public Interest', George Dominguez of the Ciba-Geigy Corporation concludes that:

First and foremost it would seem that business must face squarely the issue of transferring itself from the silent majority to the vocal majority. The key action ingredient is involvement – with all that that rather simple word implies. Such involvement means not only review, analysis, and understanding, but communication of the corporate position whenever and wherever this is both appropriate and desirable.

The area for possible involvement and action where business has the least chance of success, in the short term at least, is that of state ownership of industry. This process rests in a political rather than economic or even social logic, and the only way to stem this particular tide is to educate and change the direction of public opinion. So long as state ownership of industrial enterprise is not only acceptable to public opinion but is virtually demanded by it in some instances, there is little business can do in its relations with government beyond an involvement in political and ideological rhetoric – and industry has proved itself a poor match for the politician in this area to date.

Affecting government policy through effecting a change in public opinion is anything but a short-term task – and in many countries of Europe it is already past the eleventh hour. If a case can be made for the preservation of business free enterprise, now is the very latest date at which it should be made. Arguments must rest primarily in provable social and economic fact, but business enterprise protagonists cannot entirely ignore the power of rhetoric that has been so much a part of the antagonists' weaponry in the debate thus far.

As just one example, take the phrase 'private enterprise', that is to say, industrial enterprise owned collectively by members of the public, as opposed to 'public industry', that which is owned in effect privately by a single entity called the State.

Private enterprise in the commonly accepted use of the phrase, except for family-owned businesses, is actually no more private than British 'public schools' are public. The phrase 'private enterprise' came into the English language at a time when it carried an entirely positive and non-controversial connotation. Now, in Europe, it has been overtaken by political events and is presented as a manifestation of an élitist society that Europeans apparently no longer want any part of. State ownership of industrial enterprise side-tracks rather than solves the problem in this context under the guise of transforming 'private enterprise' into 'public industry'. There is a perfectly valid and real discussion point on this issue alone.

The area in which business enterprise must and can have effective impact is that of the legislative and regulatory process of government. Businessmen must sanction and encourage sensible and constructive legislation, and purposefully attack unconstructive and unproductive regulation that is perhaps designed to satisfy a momentary political need. That industry has failed in this task in the past is not much in doubt. The question is, is this a result of the irresistible force of political movement or the lack of an immovable will on the part of industrial enterprise? The answer seems to be that businessmen are so absorbed by the immediate problems of running an enterprise from day to day that they have little time to do more than react to and complain about government impositions. This is coupled with a reluctance to get involved in the political process, which seems to most businessmen to be both cumbersome and at odds with the more urgent and tangible needs of operating an enterprise.

Business and government are now inescapably bound together by the principles of Europe's emerging industrial democracy, but each is still guided by very different frames of reference. While, as Britain's former prime minister Harold Wilson once said, 'a week in politics is a long time', the government machine is a ponderous beast and the process that leads to the enactment of a piece of legislation is often very long indeed.

HOW CAN INDUSTRY ACT?

In terms of influencing the legislative process, the problem can be complex. Legislation at both the national and the international levels goes through several processes before it becomes law or regulation. It should be the ambition of industrial management to exercise an influence as far back as possible in that process. Legislation begins in embryo as an idea or political ambition; it progresses through various stages of private and eventually public discussion until it becomes a form of 'conventional wisdom'. The step from this to government policy is a relatively short one. Industry must therefore strive to exercise an influence at those stages before that of 'conventional wisdom' and preferably before that of public debate. By this stage the key participants in the development of government policy have dug themselves into a position from which it would be publicly embarrassing for them to extricate themselves.

To start with, the businessman should value the fact that in this instance he holds some trump-cards. After all, he knows his own company and probably his own industry better than any civil servant or politician. He should know better than anyone what can reasonably be expected in the way of social and economic performance from a given company or industry. He appreciates in far greater detail than any government official what practical forces are at work to influence that performance. The businessman is therefore in a prime position to exercise a constructive and mature influence over the shape of government policy that affects its substantial input to the general wellbeing of society.

To quote Confucius, 'The essence of knowledge is, having it, to apply it.'

In most cases government welcomes constructive advice from any source. No government develops bad or irrelevant policy deliberately. But it does not always have sufficient faith in the credibility of industry's viewpoint, especially if this is presented in confrontation during a period of public debate on some pending measure. Business leadership must therefore get behind the scene of government and know how and where to tap into the system at a stage where it can exercise reasoned persuasion. This applies to both the political and executive branches of government.

The process starts with knowing something of the power structure of national government, which differs quite considerably from country to country in Europe, and of knowing who the key players are in relation to the business viewpoint to be represented.

In some countries the structure of government is somewhat complex, especially in trying to determine where the bases of real power lie. Take France, for example. There is, to begin with, a subtle and shifting balance of power between the president of the Republic and the prime minister, even though the latter is appointed by the former. The president (who in

France has very much more real power than that position commands in any other European republic) has a highly skilled personal team of specialists and technocrats advising him at the Elysée Palace. The prime minister and other ministers in the government (who are frequently not elected politicians) have their own private political staffs that exert considerable influence over policy, as well as their administrative staff in the various ministries. The latter exercise a different kind of power because of their very permanence whatever the change in the fortunes of their political masters. In a country like Britain, on the other hand, the structure is much simpler. The head of state has no political power, and there is no army of personal political staffs for government ministers.

Tapping into the political power points of government at the national level is very largely a matter of personal contact. For many companies, either because of their size or the nature of their business, there is usually at least one natural point of contact. This is especially true for those companies that have government as a customer, and those whose activities naturally exercise a considerable impact on the nation's economy or, increasingly, the environment. But these natural points of contact will not be sufficient in themselves if one accepts the need for a company to have a relationship with government that will enable it to influence future legislation, satisfy government's legitimate information needs and determine what government perceives to be its needs of business in shaping the future of industrial policy. To achieve these objectives the businessman must seek out and develop a productive relationship with a number of different power bases in both the political and executive branches of government.

Contact at the political level is usually very much easier to achieve than at the executive level. Politicians are expected to hold and express an informed, if biased, viewpoint. The executive branch has to remain non-political and should not be seen to possess any view or bias. For this reason civil servants are much more reluctant to have a 'relationship' with industry, unless their function actually requires it.

Identification of the power-points that a particular company should attempt to influence, in addition to the natural points of contact we have already referred to, begins with a systematic assessment of its existing and future business activity. This makes it possible to identify which aspects of it are likely to bring the company within the sphere of government interest. For example, if a company plans to expand its activities in areas of high technology, especially if this is in an industry of national strategic importance like defence or telecommunications, it knows that areas of likely government interest in Europe will centre on the company's role:

1. as a government supplier (the natural point of contact);
2. as a potential exporter;
3. as a potential employer, perhaps in a designated development area;
4. as a possible recipient of development grants;
5. as a potential threat, in the case of a subsidiary of a foreign-owned corporation, to indigenous industry in the same technological area;
6. as a possible candidate for future nationalization or government control through some other means.

To avoid unnecessary misunderstanding, and indeed to enhance the success of the proposed expansion, the company in question must communicate with a number of politicians and government departments to cover these key points.

A company in the chemical industry or some other with a potential impact on the environment, or a company that can anticipate that changes in its production technology will greatly reduce its future need for manual labour, will need to establish a relationship with a different set of government power-points. In every case, however, contact and communication should be established well in advance of any potential threat from government policy or action.

All major companies should make it their business to stay in close direct touch with government thinking on the industries in which they are involved and so avoid unpleasant legislative and other surprises. Companies operating within the European Community should also keep a weather eye on legislation affecting their industry in other European Community countries, and keep a finger on the pulse of the European Commission. The legal standards of other Community countries may well become the norms set for all in Community directives.

Companies that take government relations seriously in Europe include IBM, Ford, Fiat, Siemens and Philips. They have already developed streamlined systems of monitoring and surveillance of government activity at both national and European Community levels. They make a great effort to keep both the political and executive branches of government well informed on the activities and developments of themselves and their industries as a whole. Some companies with more limited resources do almost as effective a job in government relations and have two advantages over those that do not. First, they have an opportunity to influence government policy constructively. Second, they are able to adapt to the needs of new legislation well in advance of its becoming a requirement. But the companies that have effective government relations in Europe can be counted on the fingers of a very few hands. The rest are doing little to promote the understanding and freedom that industry as a whole would wish to have, and even less to help themselves as individual enterprises with more than the short-term in mind.

Many companies that are unable to undertake this activity themselves, perhaps because of their small size, use consultants and industry associations. The latter, in general, are reasonably effective at gathering information but are frequently weak on action because of the complex and cumbersome decision-making processes to which most are subject. Indeed, the difficulty in most circumstances of being able to develop a potent industry position on any given issue is a severely limiting factor in bringing any industrial weight to bear on government activity. However, this is an added reason for large companies to do a more effective job individually. It is also an added reason for medium-sized and smaller companies that cannot undertake this activity themselves to ensure that the industry associations to which they subscribe do this on their behalf with optimum effectiveness.

In Germany only trade and industry associations are permitted to be officially registered as representatives to the federal government in Bonn. Nearly 800 are listed. While large companies also have their own unregistered representatives in Bonn, German industry has largely mastered the art of investing business and industry associations with the power and data to act effectively on its behalf. This applies to its relations with both national government and the European Community. The rest of European industry must strive to achieve the same standards of effectiveness.

Lobbying (which is a much more subtle activity in Europe than in America), provided it is restricted to areas of information, argument and advocacy, is a perfectly legitimate business tool for influencing legislation. So, too, are other areas of communication such as use and encouragement of the media to contribute to or initiate public debate on specific issues. Management should use the press, media of its own creation such as external magazines, annual reports and media advertising, and also its communication channels with employees, to underpin its more private representations to government officials.

One of the more effective tools of company relations with government, and a company's or industry's ability to influence government policy, is that of self-regulation. This is especially true in the context of recommended voluntary guidelines, and self-imposed codes of conduct. Company codes of conduct have achieved a ready and fashionable acceptance over the past few years. Unfortunately, too many of them have been constructed more for the benefit of public relations and the press release than for communication and action within the corporation itself. Self-regulatory codes of conduct have a value, indeed an important value, if they are openly self-policed. This means that management must report at least to government (and preferably more publicly) on its conduct within the established guidelines. The absence of effective self-regulation leads inevitably to imposed legislation.

MULTINATIONALS

A particular target for recent government attention and regulation has been the multinational corporation. This is a perfect target because it is by definition 'foreign', mostly big, and seemingly impersonal. Attitudes to multinational corporations among senior businessmen, professional people and civil servants are highly critical in some European countries according to a 1975 survey carried out by Landell Mill Associates. Table 7 illustrates the point. Table 8 indicates that the same sample (the research was based on 500 personal interviews in each country) feels that international business should be still further regulated.

With the public and political pressures that these statistics imply, the 1976 OECD guidelines for international investment and multinational enterprises have received a deplorably low level of public acceptance from corporations operating in the free world. The guidelines call for the following in terms of disclosure of information:

Enterprise should, having due regard to their nature and relative size in the economic context of their operations and to requirements of business confidentiality and to cost, publish in a form suited to improve public understanding a sufficient body of factual information on the structure, activities and policies of the enterprise as a whole, as a supplement, in so far as necessary for this purpose, to information to be disclosed under the national law of the individual countries in which they operate. To this end, they should publish within reasonable time limits, on a regular basis, but at least annually, financial statements and other pertinent information relating to the enterprise as a whole, comprising in particular:

i) the structure of the enterprise, showing the name and location of the parent company, its main affiliates, its percentage ownership, direct and indirect, in these affiliates, including shareholdings between them;

ii) the geographical areas* where operations are carried out and the principal activities carried on therein by the parent company and the main affiliates;

iii) the operating results and sales by geographical area and the sales in the major lines of business for the enterprise as a whole;

iv) significant new capital investment by geographical area and, as far as practicable, by major lines of business for the enterprise as a whole;

v) a statement of the sources and uses of funds by the enterprise as a whole;

vi) the average number of employees in each geographical area;

vii) research and development expenditure for the enterprise as a whole;

viii) the policies followed in respect of intra-group pricing;

ix) the accounting policies, including those on consolidation, observed in compiling the published information.

This level of disclosure represents a commonly acceptable minimum for most of the governments involved. It also is, or was, a classic opportunity for business to close ranks publicly behind a set of not unreasonable standards. This never happened, except in the case of a very few corporations.

Industry has much to learn in its dealings with government and the process of legislation. Failure to do so in the past has lead to unnecessarily punitive legislation and a dangerous shift in government and public attitudes to industrial enterprise. Today's circumstances call for more than reaction. They call for intelligent preaction, open involvement in the process of government, strong advocacy of industry's viewpoint, and a lot more goodwill and self-regulation.

For the purpose of the guideline on disclosure of information the term 'geographical area' means groups of countries or individual countries as each enterprise determines it appropriate in its particular circumstances. While no single method of grouping is appropriate for all enterprises or for all purposes, the factors to be considered by an enterprise would include the significance of operations carried out in individual countries or areas as well as the effects on its competitiveness, geographic proximity, economic affinity, similarities in business environments and the nature, scale and degree of interrelationship of the enterprises' operations in the various countries.

Table 7

Attitudes towards multinational corporations based on responses to
five questions related to their perceived social and economic impact in
the various countries

Country	Pro	Neutral	Anti
	%	%	%
Spain	2	3	94
France	6	4	90
Italy	9	3	87
Denmark	14	5	81
Belgium	15	6	77
West Germany	17	5	78
Switzerland	18	6	76
Austria	20	6	72
Sweden	24	7	67
Norway	36	4	58
Netherlands	41	7	51
Britain	44	12	43

For each country, the balance to 100 per cent is made up of these who had no opinion.

Table 8

Changes desired in the level of government control over multinational
corporations (for comparison, the changes desired in the level of
government control of business in general are given in brackets)

Country	More	The same	Less
	%	%	%
Spain	76 (64)	14 (12)	2 (5)
Italy	68 (57)	15 (24)	4 (10)
Denmark	63 (27)	22 (41)	9 (26)
France	56 (28)	18 (29)	5 (30)
Belgium	53 (36)	28 (38)	7 (16)
West Germany	51 (25)	36 (48)	7 (20)
Austria	46 (19)	33 (55)	5 (18)
Norway	43 (20)	37 (38)	11 (37)
Switzerland	41 (19)	44 (63)	2 (11)
Sweden	38 (18)	48 (58)	6 (16)
Netherlands	33 (18)	40 (47)	11 (24)
Britain	23 (9)	47 (31)	16 (56)

For each country, the balance to 100 per cent is made up of those who had no opinion.

5

Stockholders and Investors

It could be said that the minimal role of the stockholder in providing crucial new working and investment capital reduces the need for industry to communicate with the group at all beyond legal requirements – at least as far as Europe is concerned. But in Europe especially, a powerful argument can be made for new efforts to ensure the widest possible ownership of business enterprise.

Of all the people with whom the businessman has to deal, stockholders are among the best served with information. In most countries this is ensured by law, and also by the rules and practice of the Stock Exchange.

The main reason for this is an historical one. When business enterprise first became subject to statute, and when institutions like the stock exchange were formed, the owners of a company were almost the only group outside the area of actually making and selling goods that management needed to contact on a regular basis. Issuing equity was a normal method of raising capital with which to operate a business.

But things have changed. Before we examine the information needs and expectations of the stockholder in Europe, we should look briefly at his character and role today.

CHARACTER OF STOCKHOLDERS

In comparing Europe and the United States, the stockholder is the exception to the trend towards a greater participative role in industry that is a characteristic of government and labour. Today roughly one American in ten owns company stock. These investors participate actively and directly in the market, and show up in their hundreds at annual stockholder's meetings. In Europe a very much smaller and dwindling number of individuals owns company stock, the markets are much less active than in America, and the annual stockholders' meeting usually attracts a sparse attendance unless the company is in actual trouble.

Ownership and trading of company stock is the very essence of American-style capitalism. The status of the individual stockholder in the prevailing economic system has remained largely undiminished over the past decades, notwithstanding the greatly increased role of the large institutional stockholder. In Europe the individual stockholder is in a weak position and is perhaps an endangered species. In most of Europe, industry that is not in the hands of individual families is increasingly being acquired by pension funds, insurance companies, the banks and the state.

Europeans who continue to invest in company stock (as opposed to the more tangible attractions of land, buildings, gold and art) tend to do so indirectly. European stockowners are not active participators as a rule. They turn their funds over to money managers for long-term investment, and leave it up to 'the professionals' to ensure the sums add up in their favour on the day of reckoning.

There has also been a noticeable increase in recent years in the amount of European money being invested in American stocks. For example, some 8–10 per cent of daily trading on the New York Stock Exchange now comes from Europe, and of that perhaps 40 per cent from Switzerland. Much of it is 'black money' and not held by or identified with the individuals who actually own it. Most of it is handled through banks and investment houses.

'The increase in European ownership of US common stock is hardly surprising,' says James Kuhn, who runs a consultancy in Europe that specializes exclusively in European stockholder and investor relations, primarily for American corporations:

> Investment in the United States market has several advantages over European markets – the political and economic environment, the liquidity and full financial disclosure characteristics. The attraction to the United States' corporation of European stockholders is that they invest for the long term – they don't dump their holdings on the short term swings.

But private investors are much less important than they used to be to the actual operation of a business. One main reason for this is that they provide very little of the new working capital that companies need. In most of Europe, and indeed America too, the provision of new working capital comes from debt, mortgages, bonds and the like, rather than new equity. According to statistics prepared by American investment advisers Siff Oakly Marks Inc., the role of new equity, in terms of total funds generated internally and externally for working capital and fixed investment needs, is currently running at roughly 4 per cent in America. The figures for European countries, while much less available, are probably comparable. The situation in Europe, however, is complicated by the role of state funding, and the possible exception of Britain where high interest rates and the structure of the capital market make the issue of new equity more attractive.

'On the European side of the Atlantic investments are complicated by political factors, and questions of national confidence, as well as economic and structural factors,' says Yves Oltramare, who is a general partner of the Swiss bank Lombard Odier & Co. and has considerable international experience:

Take Italy for example – over fifty per cent of the economy is already indirectly nationalised and within months of the June 1976 general election, which saw substantial Communist gains, all the money that could leave the country had left. The market is at rock bottom. On the other hand, while Britain's economy may not have been in much better shape at that time, the country had a structural advantage over the rest of Europe from the investor's standpoint. Although 25 per cent of British industry is owned by the state, nearly 4,000 stocks are listed on British exchanges, compared with fewer than 200 in Italy and well under 1,000 in France (the nearest rival to Britain in Europe). As a result, Britain's historical strength in the international financial community has been a decided advantage in the recent economic difficulties. The extent to which industrial democracy and worker participation influence corporate policies can also be worrying for those who make investment decisions; but it is interesting to note that there is no shortage of capital in Germany where worker participation has been an integral part of industrial relations for decades. Actually, economic stability is a much more crucial factor than the colour of a country's politics.

State ownership is widespread in Europe. Apart from direct nationalization of some industries, natural resources and utilities (electricity, gas and water), the state participates in industrial ownership through holding companies like Italy's IRI, Spain's INI and Britain's NEB. In some countries too, a considerable amount of indirect investment in industry is controlled through state-owned banks and insurance companies.

Yet another key factor in the ownership of European industry has been the American multinational corporation. In the 1950s and 1960s especially, American corporations invested heavily in European industry through both acquisition and internal expansion – giving rise in 1967 to Jean-Jacques Servan Schrieber's 'The American Challenge' which achieved such popular credibility in Europe at that time.

Basically, then, European stockholders fall into three categories:

1. the monopoly stockholder, in the case of nationalized industries, family-owned companies and those wholly owned by a national or multinational parent company;
2. the large institutional stockholder, such as the pension funds, banks, trades unions and again the state;
3. the small individual stockholder, who invests inherited or acquired personal wealth.

ATTRACTING NEW STOCKHOLDERS

Tapping these resources (apart from those that are owned or controlled by the state) for investment in the United States is not particularly complex. Achieving an understanding with the potential sharebuyer is of very much less significance than an effective relationship with the portfolio advisers and fund managers, security analysts and economics departments of European banks. Once the key individuals have been identified, this is largely a matter of giving them the same degree of attention and information as if they were actually in the United States. The first major objective is to have one's company in the 'master list' that virtually all the major banks have of stocks that the portfolio manager can select from. Sending an investor relations manager or even a high-powered team of corporate officers round the major banks of Europe every other year is clearly useless on its own. It has to be backed up by a system that will ensure a prompt and full flow of relevant financial, industry and company data – both directly and through analysts in American brokerage firms (a key information source for security analysts in Europe following American companies).

According to a recent study carried out by Opinion Research Corporation for the Continental Group, American stock specialists in Europe rate information sources in the following order of priority:

1. annual reports to stockholders;
2. written reports of analysts in other firms;
3. news, business, financial and professional publications;
4. quarterly reports;
5. conversations with analysts in other firms;
6. management presentations at meetings called by brokerage firms;
7. copies of formal presentation made by management to analysts.

The same study indicated that most US stock specialists in Europe keep relatively few factors in mind when evaluating the investment attractiveness of a company. The six points they emphasize in the order of priority are:

1. quality of earnings;
2. competitive position;
3. estimate of future earnings;
4. competence of management;
5. past earnings record;
6. growth potential of markets served.

So far as European industry is concerned, management has some important decisions to take on its relationship with stockholders, and on the level and type of communication required to sustain that relationship.

European companies, even the very biggest of them, are frequently reluctant to go beyond their national boundaries for funds, even when they are legally able to do so. This is part of the economic national chauvinism that persists as a characteristic of the Continent. So stockholder relations for European companies remain primarily a part of the national environment. It could be said that the minimum role of the stockholder in providing crucial new working and investment capital reduces the need for industry to communicate with the group at all beyond legal requirements – at least as far as Europe is concerned.

But in Europe especially a powerful argument can be made for new efforts to ensure the widest possible ownership of business enterprise on two counts.

1. The general threat to any form of freedom, including freedom of enterprise, is a concentration of power in too few hands. A large body of individual stockholders can act as a counter-balance to powerful institutional investors, government and trades unions.

2. If Europe's participative form of industrial democracy is to develop
    logically, it must include participation by employees in the ownership
    of the company for which they work as well as in management
    decisions.

These points are highly political. Both are anathema to the extreme
Left, the only possible concession it is prepared to make to the second
point being worker ownership through trade unions. Much of the political
Right, on the other hand, favours the former but is reluctant to embrace
the latter because it *seems* like some form of socialism.

Resolution of the first point requires a number of economic, political
and structural changes that will make ownership of company stock as
attractive as ownership of land, property and gold. Initiative for such
change must come from industry itself, because no political force with any
power in Europe today is likely to move in that direction voluntarily.
There is a potentially important role here for such institutions as the
investment clubs, of which there are already 16,000 in Europe. In some
countries, like France, such clubs carry tax and other advantages.

Resolution of the second point, though it may result from some
currently dormant political inspiration, could come rapidly from
individual company initiatives. Indeed, a few companies already have
schemes for worker ownership of company stock. Philip Rosenthal AG,
the German manufacturers of porcelain, glass and furniture, gives
company stock as bonus payments to its workers and allows them to
purchase additional stock at preferential prices. Almost 30,000 IBM
workers in Europe, about a third of the total number of employees, have
taken advantage of that company's scheme permitting any employee to
allocate up to 10 per cent of his earnings to buy IBM stock at a 15 per cent
discount. Companies that have employee stock-option schemes have noted
favourable shifts in employee attitudes to both the company and work.

COMPANY REPORTS

In most European countries the law insists on a basic level of reliable
financial reporting to the stockholder; although this is a relatively recent
phenomenon. 'In the late 1950s and early 1960s the first post-war
discovery of European markets resulted in vast price exaggerations which
were painfully corrected from mid-1962 through to the end of 1966,'
comments Mario Zupponi, head of European Research for the Swiss bank
Lombard Odier & Company. 'By that time corporate reporting had

become good enough to permit a fair valuation of the stocks in the various markets, and very substantial progress has been made since then.'

Europe still lags far behind American requirements for corporate disclosure of financial and other information, however, and further legislation in Europe is as certain as it is justified in today's social context. Any company that plans to remain in business for the next decade, therefore, should regard the levels of information required by law and regulation today as minimum standards rather than norms. Improved regulation on the disclosure of information should assist development of one essential prerequisitive to any increase in the constructive role of the stockholder in the participative mix of Europe's industrial democracy-stockholder confidence.

This is usually achieved in two ways. One is a history of good financial performance. The other is the stockholders' and potential investors' belief in the company's management and the future of the business in which is operates. This quality of confidence rarely springs from blind faith in either the economic system or an individual (though there are examples of company stock value relying very heavily on the calibre of the chief executive). Rather, it depends on a knowledge and understanding by the stockholder and potential investor of a company and its capabilities that can only result from the availability and comprehension of relevant information – in other words, effective communication.

This level of understanding and confidence is not achieved by an inspired company treasurer or the appointment of an investor relations consultant, though these characters may have an important role to play. It is achieved because the board of directors, and above all the chief executive, understands the need for his company to develop and sustain an ongoing rather than merely annual relationship with stockholders and investment advisers. It requires boardroom commitment and top management involvement in the development and implementation of a structured stockholder and investor relations programme.

Let us look now at some of the key information needs and expectations of the European stockholder. They certainly go far beyond the balance sheet and normal regulatory requirements, and generally fall into three categories.

1.   *Financial track record.* It is easy to say that this need is satisfied by the annual report, but this is not always so. How many chief executives can claim that they have always striven to present information in their annual report in a way that it can be most fully understood? Even within the requirements of law and regulation there remains some

scope in a few European countries for manipulation of the figures with the help of an understanding auditor, or at the very least the selective use of information to conceal or confuse reality.

2. *The company's future prospects.* Being infinitely less tangible than historical performance, this is an area that stockholders wish to have explained with completeness and conservative honesty, not with the glib optimism of a politician's election promise. In many countries now, legal and other regulatory requirements place very tight constraints on a company's freedom to comment on the future with unfounded enthusiasm; but stockholders do want to know, quite simply, what the future holds in terms of available markets, opportunities for expansion or diversification and potential problems. Any company management that can develop a reputation with stockholders for conservatively accurate forecasting is building a long-term credibility that will help sustain it in bad times and earn enthusiastic support in times of plenty.

3. *The quality and calibre of management, present and future.* This has three aspects, two closely tied to the last point. The stockholder wants to feel confident that management can plan and operate effectively for the future wellbeing of the company, and that there is sufficient depth in a company's management to assure a long-term future that is not dependent on one or two brilliant men. Thirdly, and this is a relatively new phenomenon, there is the whole area of corporate maturity and morality. If the only way management can keep the 'bottom line' healthy is to cut short-term corners and exceed the bounds of acceptable corporate behaviour, stockholders become nervous. Their nervousness is reflected in the price they will pay for a company's stock, or whether they want to hold it at all.

These simple needs and expectations are rarely satisfied in full, though the tools to do the job already exist. The primary sources of information for stockholders in general are the annual report, the media, the banks, stockbrokers and financial analysts. In the case of large institutional investors, personal and regular access to a company's top management must be added to this list; but effective stockholder relations will depend on the use of a balanced combination of communication of skills and techniques.

The need for an industrial level of communication with private and institutional investors and banks is well recognized by the European chief executives whose opinions we surveyed for this book. Banks and private stockholders were high on the list of key publics with which industry currently communicates. Indeed, apart from business and trade associations they were rated higher than any external audience. Nevertheless, many more chief executives thought companies should communicate with both groups on a more regular basis than is now the practice – by a factor of 50 per cent in the case of private stockholders. Institutional investors were much lower down the priority list of publics currently receiving company information. But nearly three times as many chief executives felt this group should receive company information on a regular basis.

The company annual report is probably one of the more classic examples of communication waste in terms of both money and opportunity. The annual report is not just a statutory requirement calling merely for a few pious words from the directors, a few well-rounded phrases on the company's activities, the odd photograph of factories and products, and a balance sheet. It is a very real opportunity for effective communication of company achievements, problems, objectives and expectations, not only to the stockholder but to a number of other key groups as well. For most medium-to-large companies the cost of producing and distributing the annual report is high – but the cost of producing one that succeeds in effective communication is not necessarily higher than the cost of one that fails.

One man who has very strong views on company annual reports is Martin Stevens, managing director of Annual Reports Ltd of London, which claims to be the only consultancy in Europe specializing exclusively in its field. 'The problem with annual reports', Stevens contends,

> is that many skills are needed for their production – accounting, legal, political, marketing, administrative, literary and creative. In far too many companies far too little time and effort is devoted to ensuring the annual report is an effective communicator – it ends up being a receptacle of potentially valuable information obscured from general comprehension by opaque presentation.

Management consultant John Humble, who has worked with a number of companies in Europe on developing systems to audit corporate social performance, believes that substantial changes in the corporate report will be required during the next decade. 'The traditional annual report to stockholders on a company's financial performance will have to be broadened to take account of industry's growing responsibilities to other groups,' says Humble.

> Companies will have to find ways of reporting on their social performance and providing a 'social impact analysis' as well as a

financial analysis. Some of the more enlightened companies are already moving in this direction; but most are at the very bottom of the learning curve.

OTHER METHODS OF COMMUNICATION

A later chapter is devoted to the media, but a word or two would be appropriate here on the specialist area affecting the stockholder. Virtually all stockholders, large or small, read some of the business press even if this is confined to the business sections of the daily and weekly media. Virtually all stockowners want to read about 'their company'. It gives them an understandable feeling of proprietary warmth. It engenders a closer sense of identity with and strengthened confidence in the company. For this to happen, of course, more is required than a press release and a few financial advertisements around the time that the annual results of the company are announced. It requires a planned and structured approach. Financial press relations take on an added significance in Europe because, as we noted earlier, the individual European stock*owner*, unlike his American counterpart, is often not the stock*holder*. Such stockowners are usually cut off from the normal flow of stockholder information, and the press is one of the few channels of communication that a company has with them.

It is, however, in its relations with banks, stockbrokers and investment analysts that a company operating in Europe can do most to promote long-term confidence in its stock. These groups are the professionals that give stockholders the 'sell', 'hold' or 'buy' advice that affects the value of a company's shares. Most company directors and managers feel fairly comfortable talking with these groups because there is a reasonably common understanding of the issues involved.

Analysts following companies in their own countries in Europe tend to apply the same criteria as those specializing in American stocks, noted earlier in this chapter. They also have to live with different accounting principles and methods, less precise regulations on disclosure and a range of national, political and economic factors. Public companies in Europe must therefore give considerable time and importance to briefing the portfolio and fund managers, security analysts and economics departments of banks in their own country.

But none of this is any substitute for face-to-face communication with the stockholder. Unfortunately, apart from the annual general meeting it is only the large institutional investors who are afforded the opportunity.

Sadly, too, few companies in Europe do enough to encourage stockholders to attend the annual meeting with the result that average attendances have dropped considerably over the past two or three decades. Perhaps it is not surprising that few chief executives enjoy or perform effectively at the annual meeting. It requires skills, in public speaking and debate, that have not been fundamental to operating a successful business enterprise in the past. They are skills, however, that can be acquired.

Industry must do a much more effective and positive job in communicating with its individual and institutional stockholders and potential investors. The influence of a large and well-informed body of interested stockholders may be crucial to the survival of free enterprise in Europe.

6

Workers and Their Representatives

The effectiveness and energy with which the individual worker will contribute to an entity larger than himself will depend upon either the extent to which he identifies with the objectives of that entity, or fear of material loss if he does not. Since the worker in Europe is largely protected from the latter, motivation must come from the former.

Industrial democracy is like beauty, in one respect at least. Its qualities lie very much in the eye of the beholder, and mean different things to different people. It certainly takes very different forms from country to country in Europe. In fact, its only common denominator is a broader sharing of influence over the shape of company policy and the affluence industry produces, coupled with the 'humanizing' of life at work. Within this three-part objective, however, there is an enormous divergence from country to country in Europe on which element the emphasis is placed and on the current pace of development.

Industrial democracy involves harmonizing and balancing the relationship between industrial ownership, government and workers. Balancing the relationship calls for new systems of communication and participation that will ensure that no one party holds most of the high cards most of the time. Harmonizing the relationship calls for a much greater level of mutual understanding and agreement on the social and economic purposes of industry.

Communication must be the instrument in this process of harmonization, and management must be the catalyst, if balance and harmony are to be achieved.

Progress towards industrial democracy in Europe has been inexorable and inevitable. In the early days, when industry took over from agriculture as the mainspring of a country's economy, there was a simple, if rather one-sided, situation where the owners of an enterprise ran it largely for their own financial interests and benefit. Workers were a resource much like any other, and governments left well alone because they lacked the means, knowledge or will to interfere. As government became more of an expression of the popular will, it began to 'participate' in the policy and activity of industry. It did this through taxation, and it used both trade and the wealth that industry created to promote both its foreign policies and the basic needs of the people that voted it into power.

Eventually, government became an active and determining participant in industry. It has achieved this through direct and indirect ownership, and a constant encroachment on industry's prerogatives via the stick and carrot of legislation and subsidy.

The social and economic levelling process that has been so much a characteristic of Europe this century, especially since World War II, has now largely satisfied the basic physical needs of man across the continent and has cleared the stage for the third element of industry's unholy trinity, the provider of labour, to join the club as a full member alongside industrial ownership and government.

Europe is well beyond the point of no return in this phase of its industrial development. While West Germany has been developing its system of worker participation since immediately after World War II, six other countries have legislated for it in some form during the past five years alone – Norway, Sweden, Denmark, Luxembourg, Austria and Holland. Britain's government-sponsored Bullock Committee has recommended another variation on the same theme, and the French seem bound to adopt yet another version as a result of its government-sponsored Sudreau Report.

The pressures in favour of workers participating directly in the development of at least some aspects of industrial policy, at local plant as well as national levels, are hard to resist. Post war events that have contributed towards this include:

1. the political drift towards democratic and other forms of socialism, both creating and justifying the need and acceptability of such concepts as industrial democracy;

2. high-paced changes in production technology that have created social unrest by reducing the need for human labour and creating a disproportionate quantity of boring and repetitive jobs on the shop floor;

3. massive changes in the quantity and quality of education (take almost any company to test the point by checking the education profile of those entering industry today with those about to retire);

4. the impact and orientation of the mass-media (television, radio, newspapers and magazines), which both reflect and in some cases lead the movement for radical social and industrial change.

Another cause-and-effect of the pressure for a more broadly based industrial democracy is the draft European Statute produced by the European Commission, which embodies a high level of worker participation at all levels of an enterprise. Added to this is the Commission's draft Fifth Directive, which is concerned solely with worker participation. Indeed, this draft directive, which may complete its gauntlet of approval stages in 1978, is likely to reflect in its final form the flexibility with which industry as a whole must approach the issue from country to country.

The Commission is backing European industrial democracy very firmly. Jack Peel, the Commission's director of industrial relations, notes:

> The first quarter of this century has been described as an era of unbridled industrial capitalism, the second quarter being marked by totalitarianism and war (a consequence of the breakdown of the old industrial order and the mass unemployment which *laissez-faire* economics could not cure). The third quarter was a boom period which, although ending in stagnation and inflation, reflected a desire to prevent a recurrence of mass unemployment without resorting to fascism or war. The fourth quarter, which we have now entered, can be either a positive and creative alternative to 'stagflation' or a grim and disastrous counter-stroke, as the second was to the first. Industrial democracy has a key role in Europe's economic revival and ultimately in the defence of democracy as we know it. Either we make industrial democracy a European fact in the near future or we slide into economic and political chaos.

In his introductory remarks to an OECD management seminar on worker participation, Deputy Secretary-General Gerard Eldin suggested that 'the business world cannot remain aloof from this movement since that would be the surest way of creating "blocked" situations and, finally, explosions that we can well do without.' In the same context he quoted the authors of France's report on the reform of the enterprise:

> Justification for reforming the enterprise should be sought less in a deficiency in its operation than in the movement of society itself. It is because our society is changing rapidly that changes in the enterprise should be speeded up. The enterprise is no more than a sub-group in the economic and social system. It cannot escape the latter's general logic.

Eldin was at pains to point out, however, that worker participation in an enterprise raised problems – and two dangers that must be avoided:

> The first would be to regard participation as a simple technique of industrial relations which can, with the wave of a magic wand, cause the disappearance of all the strains that are inherent in the existence of different categories and functions within the enterprise. To adopt such an approach would, I think, be to take the road towards serious disillusionment. The second is that under the pretext of organising fairer and better informed collaboration between the bodies responsible for different functions, we should in fact receive a confusion of responsibilities from which the enterprise would have nothing to gain.

Eldin concludes on these issues that

> it is only by avoiding these two dangers that we can hope that the effort of participation will not only bring about an improvement in the social climate but also (and because of this) greater economic effectiveness within the firm and more harmonious development of our society.

The argument that effective worker participation can contribute fully towards greater economic effectiveness is perhaps best demonstrated in Europe by the example of West Germany, and outside Europe by the example of Japan. American businessmen frequently complain that it takes 'for ever' to get a decision out of Japanese management and wonder how such apparent slowness of response can have contributed favourably towards that country's so-called 'postwar economic miracle'. The comparison is made with the American manager who takes decisions fast. The short answer to the question is, of course, that so many people 'down the line' have been involved in the process of taking a business decision in a Japanese firm that implementation of the decision is assured. When the American manager takes a fast decision on his own he can be reasonably certain that twenty other managers will have different views, which they will strive to have factored into its implementation, necessarily resulting in delays and compromise.

The United States has largely held fast to the basic concepts of capitalism and the free market economy. Europe has favoured the mixed economy and a participative form of industrial democracy, with government exercising considerable influence over the strategy and policy of industry. Growth, profit and earnings-per-share remain the simple yardsticks by which most Americans judge a company to be successful; while in Europe, industry is expected to have broader and more socially oriented objectives, with profit (to many a misunderstood and somehow 'dirty' word) regarded as a means to an end rather than an end in itself. In Europe the participative form of industrial democracy, with workers as well as government participating in the development of many areas of company policy, is a well established pattern; while in the United States the concept of worker participation, beyond stock-option plans and a few experiments in workers sharing company profits, is practically an un-American activity. More prominent issues in America have been equal employment opportunities for women and for minority groups. In America, too, the rights of the individual are considered, in practice, far superior to the welfare of society as a whole. In Europe political priorities and aspirations have led most of its nations in the other direction.

Of course, these few examples oversimplify the issues involved. There is no one American philosophy any more than there is a common philosophy for Europe; but the basic principles are valid. It is not our purpose here to draw conclusions as to which represents the better philosophy because this inevitably will depend on the personal perspectives, priorities and fortunes of the individual. Each philosophy has been developed, moreover, to meet very different social and industrial circumstances. But these factors have exercised a profound effect on the character and performance of business enterprise on either side of the Atlantic.

Clearly, the evolution of European industrial democracy will have some vital consequences for the industrial strength and viability both of Europe as a whole and of the nations it comprises. The cynics, especially in American industrial management, see the process undermining the flexibility and ultimately the competitiveness of European industry. The optimists regard this view as merely self-deceiving conservatism. The fact is that social peace must underlie any long-term competitive strength and, using days lost per thousand employees per year as one measure of productive social peace, there is a strong correlation with the practice of worker participation.

Germany, the Netherlands, Norway, Sweden and Denmark each have historical rates no more than 1/17 of Italy's, 1/15 of Canada's, 1/14 of the United States, 1/13 of Ireland's, 1/7 of Britain's, 1/4 of France's and 1/3 of Belgium's. Even allowing for creative statistical reporting, there's no denying the message [comments Dr Jerry O'Connell, a senior faculty member of the Centre d'Etudes Industrielles in Geneva and a long-standing authority on European industrial democracy]. Putting the 'producer' role in harmony with man's other roles is an economic coup in the battle with communism.

Although it is too early to draw definite conclusions from the data, worker participation may be one of the few sure ways of ensuring that business enterprise is allowed to continue in anything like a form we recognize today. Far from ringing the death knell of business enterprise, it may prove to be a primary course towards its salvation – the known alternative being outright government ownership of industry through communism or some other form of collectivism. But for this new order of life to work, as we have already pointed out, European industry must achieve a new balance and harmony among its participants that depends on a sharing of common ground that can only result from goodwill, a free flow of information and ideas, and effective communication. It cannot work if industrial management is oriented primarily to providing the stockholder with dividends, while government regards the purpose of industry as fuelling the economy and balancing the national budget, and workers insist that industry's primary objective is to provide interesting and fulfilling jobs for all. These often conflicting ambitions, each justifiable in themselves perhaps, must be brought into closer harmony.

NATIONAL CHARACTERISTICS

The evolutionary process towards industrial democracy, and the information needs and expectations of industry's newest active participant, must be seen in the context of the individual national environment. Worker participation is one of the more classic examples of entrenched differences between the nations of Europe. These differences highlight the cultural and ethnic diversity of Europe and some of the more permanent scars of history.

The shape of industrial democracy in those countries that have legislated for it so far varies according to three main determining factors:

1. the structure and strength of the trades union movement;

2. ethnic characteristics of the country's population;

3. the economic and social circumstances in which it is introduced and developed.

The structure and strength of the trades union movement is a key determinant, as it conditions the answer to the fundamental question of who will 'participate' on behalf of the work force. A quick look at Germany, the Netherlands and Britain will illustrate the point.

In Germany, less than 40 per cent of labour is unionized. Unions are based on industrial sectors (it is rare to find more than one union operating in one company). As a consequence worker participation is based on representatives elected directly by the workers at local level to the factory works council. These in turn elect representatives to a company works council (in the case of a company with more than one factory location), and this body elects representatives to the company's supervisory board of directors. It will be noted that the legal constitution of a company in West Germany calls for a two-tier board – a supervisory board that controls policy, and a management board that implements policy and runs the company on a day-to-day basis. By participating at the supervisory board level, worker representatives influence policy while retaining credibility with those they represent by not getting directly involved in actually managing the enterprise. It is perhaps interesting to note that most elected representatives to works councils are trade union members; but this is despite rather than because of the electoral system. It is rather because the trades unions ensure that their members in a company are sufficiently well educated in business practice, through their own schools and universities, to be self-evidently the best representatives of worker interests.

In the Netherlands a little over 40 per cent of labour is unionized. The trades union movement is politically strong, highly centralized, and based on political ideology and religion as well as industry sectors. Thus, it is not uncommon for a company to have to work with two or three unions. The worker participation legislation in the Netherlands as a consequence calls for union representation at board level and an entirely separate system of elected joint labour–management works councils at factory level. Being a much less integrated system than the German model, there tends to be more polarization than harmony of views among the 'participants' at board level.

In Britain about half of labour is unionized. The trades union movement is politically very powerful, and is based traditionally on individual crafts and trades rather than on industries or competing political and religious ideologies. As a consequence a company may have to deal with a dozen different powerful unions which may be in conflict with each other as well as with management. The Bullock Committee recommendations, calling for parity representation for trades unions on the single-tier company board of directors, is a strong reflection of the trades union setup in Britain. Indeed, until very recently the British trades union movement was hostile or just apathetic to the concept of worker participation, and some of it remains so (in common with much of the trades union movement in France and Italy, where respectively a little over 20 per cent and 30 per cent of labour is unionized and is largely communist-controlled). And the Bullock plan seems to be more concerned with trade union control than with worker participation.

Ethnic characteristics play a central role in worker participation, too, though these are much less tangible, and subject to personal perspectives. It would seem obvious, however, that the Scandinavian propensity to avoid conflict has a constructive impact on industrial harmony and the emphasis on the 'humanization' of life at work. Equally, the tendency of the German to seek collective and orderly solutions must also have a positive impact. The British social 'caste' system, and the emphasis placed by trades unions on protecting their individual power and influence, on the other hand, are not necessarily conducive to harmony among industry's 'participants'. Equally, the comparatively fiery Latin temperament and the emotional conflict that tends to characterize the politics of countries like France, Italy and Spain must present some measure of obstacle to industrial harmony and the willingness of all participants to pull in the same direction.

Economic and social circumstances are also key conditioning factors in the development of worker participation because they govern the pace and to some extent the emphasis on its introduction at various levels. For example, worker participation was introduced in West Germany at a time when there was a strong sense of national reorientation and change. Its postwar development took place in a period of industrial expansion when the economy was flexible enough to handle the burden of experiment and some inevitable mistakes. Additionally, because the development was pioneering in uncharted industrial waters, there were no great external pressures for early results. None of these factors applies to any of the European countries now turning the corner into industrial democracy.

But none of these factors is a reason to reverse the current course of events, even if this were possible (which it almost certainly is not). They are, however, factors to be considered in 'managing' the pace at which each country moves towards the final objectives of industrial democracy. In some countries it will be a question of 'more haste, less speed'.

Three lessons can be learned from the experience Europe already has with worker participation in the seven nation states that have legislated for it.

1. Worker participation should be approached as an evolutionary rather than a revolutionary milestone in the progress of industrial development.

2. It works successfully only if it is underpinned by an established system of well informed works councils (with competent trades union support) that understand the basic economics of enterprise, and that can ensure proper representation of workers' views.

3. It only works where there is a general consensus on the purpose and objectives of industry, broadly shared by workers, management, company ownership and government alike.

In fact, the whole thing stands or falls on a measure of mutual respect and understanding of both the social and economic purpose and limitations of industry. This can only result from a continuous flow of information and ideas, and a readiness at all levels of industry to be educated and to allow traditionally entrenched attitudes and values to be changed.

One of the key reasons for the success of worker participation in countries like West Germany is that worker representatives are taught the basic economics of business enterprise at schools and universities run by the trade unions, and sponsored by both government and industry as well. Worker representatives are allowed by law to spend two weeks every other year attending courses, and by the time they are elected to represent workers on the supervisory board of directors this basic level of education has been underpinned by considerable practical experience in works councils at factory and company levels. By this time their understanding and their contribution to the development of company policy can be very valuable. Company involvement in the education of workers' representatives in the context of the German model contains many lessons for management in other countries, even though the practical implementation of similar programmes elsewhere would need to be conditioned by a different set of social and economic parameters.

COMMUNICATIONS POLICY

In establishing a framework for future business practice in communicating with workers and their representatives, we shall look at some of the key aspects of the potential impact of information and the risks of communication, today's legal requirements, and finally some areas of communication that management should perhaps devote immediate attention to.

In the OECD report titled *Workers' Participation* following an international management seminar on the subject, the Organization notes in a section on information, education and training that:

The arguments against providing full information to workers fall into two categories:

1. The possible leaking of confidential information will endanger the competitive position of the enterprise.

2. Information is a source of power; providing unlimited information to workers and in particular to the union undermines the management's position in collective bargaining.

Certainly these are problem issues affecting the disclosure of some types of information to workers. But these factors should merely help set the limits of information to be disclosed, help define the individuals to be communicated with, and help the timing of the communication of highly sensitive information.

In an article published in a recent issue of *Industrial Relations,* Arthur Marsh and Roger Rosewell of Oxford University ask several pertinent questions in just one paragraph:

The general arguments in favour of disclosure are difficult to resist. It is scarcely possible to deny the virtues and likely advantages of being well informed; such a denial may all too easily appear to signify approval of ignorance and who, in a democracy, can credibly do that? Is it not better where collective bargaining is concerned that negotiations should be about facts rather than emotions? Is it not true that for any worker to give of his best that he ought to understand his role and function in the productive process? For what other purpose has the last hundred years of public education been devoted?

Perhaps the most exhaustive survey on company communication with workers to be carried out in Europe recently was the 1976 study commissioned by the Confederation of British Industry on the attitudes of shopfloor workers. In a section on the potential rewards and risks of communication, the survey showed that there is a very strong relationship between workers being well informed and having a high level of job satisfaction – with all that implies for morale, absenteeism and so forth. The well-informed in the survey were two and a half times more likely than the ill-informed to say they were satisfied with their job. The survey report also noted from other sources that well-informed employees and union negotiators are more likely to be realistic in wage negotiations, especially in relation to the ability of a firm to meet a claim. The report goes on to say:

> The study suggests that management should set strong benefits such as these against the risks inherent in employee communications. There is also the risk to be taken into account of not communicating adequately to employees. For example, it is hard to imagine pay settlements [in Britain] more damaging than those of 1974-75. The study concludes therefore, that there is no such thing as an employee communications policy that avoids risks. The challenge to management today is to manage the risks of employee communications in a positive planned fashion as professionally as it manages other aspects of its business.

The communication of relevant information through the works council structure in countries where these exist has been proved to play a key role in the prevention-rather-than-cure approach to problems on the shop floor. The dialogue that exists between management and workers through works councils, especially in countries like Germany, Sweden and Norway, is a key contributor to the low industrial strike figures referred to earlier in this chapter – not to mention questions of basic national economic stability. Problems tend to get solved before they become crises. This is perhaps especially true in the case of redundancies. In some European countries not only does the number of people to be made redundant have to be reviewed and approved by the works council or relevant union, but the identity of those individuals to be affected has to be approved as well. The system has its advantages. It avoids the situation, not untypical of countries like Britain, where redundancies are followed by hundreds or thousands of other employees going on strike in sympathy.

So far as legal requirements are concerned in the area of disclosure of information to workers and their representatives, Europe remains a patchwork of conflicts and contrasts. Most countries in Europe have laws that prescribe the type of information that must be communicated to worker representatives, and the intervals and timeliness with which it must be communicated. In Germany the issue is thoroughly well regulated, the rules are clear to all and followed by most. The law requires a broad range of social and economic data, both historical and forecast, to be communicated to worker representatives.

The new Swedish law on co-determination at work, which came into effect at the beginning of this year, contains no less than five clauses on the rights of workers to have access to company information. One states that:

> the employer shall keep the trade union to which he is bound by collective agreement continuously informed on the development of the production and economy of his business and also of the guidelines for his personnel policy. The employer shall similarly give the trade union an opportunity in so far as the union so needs in looking after the joint interests of its members in relation to the employer, to examine books, accounts and other documents which relate to the employer's business.

Within the European Community, Britain and Ireland stand alone in having no law, as yet, relating to the disclosure of information to workers and their representatives. New legislation in this area is inevitable, however, and the more enlightened enterprises have begun to meet (and possibly exceed) the likely requirements of the law. This has been especially true of multinational corporations that have experience of legislation in other countries.

Ireland represents the nadir of legislated communication with workers within the European Community. The 1963 Company's Act required public companies to send a basic level of information of historical financial performance to stockholders, and to file the same information with the Registrar of Companies so it can be inspected by members of the public. However, because this law applies only to public companies employing more than 350 workers, it ignores nearly 40,000 Irish firms, almost a quarter of which are engaged in manufacturing operations. An estimated 80 per cent of Irish workers are, as a result, employed by companies where no disclosure of information is required by the law. Additionally, Irish trades union officials complain that by no means all the 350 companies affected by the law actually file information in a time-frame that would give the information any value.

In contrast with the Irish experience and existing comprehensive legislation in countries that comprise the north-eastern segment of Western Europe, the French, however, are planning, in late 1977, to vote into law proposals from the Ministry of Labour calling for companies employing more than 300 workers to provide an annual 'social balance sheet' which would enable employees to determine changes and improvements in conditions of employment. Employers will be required to submit to the works council a 'social audit', detailing information on employment, pay, working conditions and safety, vocational training and industrial relations. The idea is that the social balance sheet will be submitted by management to the works council, which will in turn submit the balance sheet and its own comments on it to stockholders.

The scheme is criticized by French trade unions, especially the communist CGT, for doing nothing to extend legislation for the disclosure of hard data beyond that already called for under the French Labour Code, but the new law may represent more than a token move towards the ambitions of European industrial democracy.

The general drift, in France and elsewhere in Europe, is inescapably towards a much greater level of disclosure of information to workers and their representatives. This presents two serious questions for management:

1. Will the information required to be disclosed by any new law be understood in its proper context by workers and their representatives?

2. Should a company attempt to anticipate these legal requirements by establishing systems of communication and the provision of information in advance?

The answer to this second question must logically be 'yes' if the problems inherent in the first are to be avoided. This brings us to the final point of this chapter, which is to determine the areas of communication with workers and their representatives that management of enterprises in Europe should perhaps devote immediate attention to.

AREAS OF COMMUNICATION

In addition to the requirement of the law (actual or pending), management must decide for itself first of all with whom it will communicate. The law may, depending on the country, require specific information on redundancies, factory closures, new investments and the like to be communicated to trades union officials in advance of management actions. However, management must also ask itself if it wants to rely exclusively on this channel for feeding information to its workers, or if it wants to establish (or simply retain) direct contact with its work force on such key issues. The Confederation of British Industry research referred to earlier in this chapter, for example, showed clearly that management was a 'preferred source' for a variety of information by shopfloor workers. Additionally only one in ten had any objection to direct communication from management.

The effectiveness and energy with which the individual worker will contribute to an entity larger than himself will depend upon either the extent to which he identifies with the objectives of that entity, or his fear of material loss if he does not. Since the worker in Europe is largely protected from the latter, motivation must come from the former.

Given management desire to communicate with workers to achieve this identity and its resulting benefits, what areas of information should be communicated, and how should that communication be effected? Types of information of relevance to workers fall broadly into two categories:

1. information about the factory in which they work and the company they work for;
2. information about the social and economic environment in which the company operates.

In both cases, the information must be prepared in a context that has some direct bearing on the life or future of the individual worker it is being communicated to. Let us take company profits as an example. Achieving a general understanding of what profits are, what they are used for, and their vital role in any economic system is one of the information areas to which management in most of Europe needs to give very urgent attention.

Profits are characterized by the extreme political Left as the cream that industrial ownership/management extracts from the milk of a worker's labour. And while few workers accept such extravagant overstatement, most have a grossly inflated concept of the level of profits and the uses to which they are put. Why? Because in most of Europe profits tend to be news once a year, and are publicized by a company largely for the benefit of stockholders in absolute and frequently substantial terms. Few companies take the trouble to explain to their workers how the sum of their profits relate in proportion to, for example, wages and salaries, or investment in new plant, equipment and research. A worker will inevitably have a distorted view of profits if all he knows about them is that they total millions, or thousands of millions of dollars, pounds, deutsche marks or francs. When he knows that his company's net profits amount to 4 or 5 per cent of company sales, 10–12 per cent of wages, or a quarter of what the company has paid in taxes and social contributions, then he gets some feeling of the true dimensions of profit. When he also knows that not all of this is paid to stockholders, much of it being retained for reserves, new investments or whatever (and what this means in terms of job security and even future expansion), the issue of profit begins to loose its emotional sting.

But explanation of profit must be taken a stage further, and management must help workers understand the painful but real consequences of making a loss – preferably before this situation becomes imminent.

These issues begin to bring the basic economics of business enterprise into proper perspective and provide a credible explanation of the inter-relationship of the providers of labour, capital and social direction.

In addition to explaining and defending the basic principles of business enterprise, management must do a more effective job of explaining its individual position and strategy within the system. This involves management necessarily in a fairly public forecast of its targets and inevitably in a subsequent need to justify why these may not have been fully met. Admissions of this kind do not come easily to anyone, least of all to the manager whose credibility is at stake. Yet within the context of Europe's emerging industrial democracy it must be so. Issues that management must explain to workers in a context that is relevant to them should include, for example:

1. a factory closure: why is it necessary and why could it not have been avoided; what will its consequences be for workers in other factories; what is the company doing to help those workers who are directly affected?

2. the opening of a new factory: why did the company choose to open a new factory rather than expand existing facilities; what impact will the new factory have on other company factories and their workers?

3. the state of the company's order book: if it is healthy, what does it mean in terms of job security and the need or opportunity for overtime; does it mean the company can afford to pay higher wages, and if not why not? If it is unhealthy, why is this and what is being done to improve the situation; what is the likely effect on future job security?

4. the company's economic and social impact: this becomes especially relevant when applied to impact on the local community of an individual factory. What does the company contribute (work, wages, training, perhaps also recreational facilities), and what does it extract (especially in the environmental area)?

In some European countries, companies are required by law to communicate much of this type of information to worker representatives, but management must also seriously consider the likely advantages of communicating it also directly to workers in general. In normal circumstances, provided it is handled with sensitivity, this can be achieved without antagonizing workers' representatives, and indeed may serve to strengthen that relationship.

The economic and social objectives of a company, the dependence of one upon the other, and management's strategy to meet them must clearly be understood by workers if they are to contribute fully towards their achievement. Management must therefore communicate effectively with those directly involved. This way everyone knows where they are being led and what is required to reach that destination. Here again, the objectives must be explained in terms that relate to the lives of the individual workers upon whom management relies for their achievement. If the destination itself cannot be explained as a justifiable ambition to workers and their representatives, the problem is not one of communication.

So far as vehicles of communication are concerned, management has a number of options within three basic channels:

1. trades unions or other official worker representatives;
2. the established internal chain of command down through management and supervisory levels to the shop floor;
3. communication media that cut across these formal channels (e.g. employee annual reports, employee newspapers, company bulletin boards, etc.).

Each of these channels individually have limitations. The first two frequently act as strong filters, albeit in different ways and with different motives. Both are likely to restrict the dissemination of some information it has access to, while embellishing others. One effective method of guarding against the worst excesses of this is to let each know that they are not the only channel being used to communicate with workers. Both of these channels rely on the strength and credibility of personal relationships within and especially at the receiving end of the communication chain, and on the personal effectiveness in communication skills of a great number of individuals. If the relationships are right and communication skills effective, both channels will prove to be very potent indeed.

The third channel of communication contains a number of different communication vehicles, each having the advantage over the other two channels of being much more controllable, and the disadvantage of being relatively impersonal. They seldom provide an opportunity to test worker reaction to a given piece of communication.

In most of Europe the employee newspaper is one of the worst excesses of communication waste. Most are little more than published management bulletin boards, avoiding sensitive issues and lacking the level of credibility necessary to do an effective job of communicating anything beyond routine information. The more adventurous and enlightened companies have opened the columns of their employee newspapers to workers, their representatives, trades union officals and others who may express views that run counter to those of management. In this way the employee newspaper becomes a forum for meaningful debate on issues of concern to the people for whom it is produced. This approach requires courage on the part of management; but it can transform the employee newspaper into a credible communicator that management may need in times of crisis.

More and more companies these days are producing employee annual reports designed to explain the economic and social performance of the company in terms that are relevant and intelligible to its workers. With the increasing pressure on companies now to produce a 'social audit' report detailing their impact on society in a very broad context, it is questionable whether management is wise to permit such a diversity of reports to be produced – despite the fact that workers have as much moral right as stockholders to receive such documentation. Quite apart from the high costs involved, there is the danger of at least appearing not to speak with one voice and of being discriminatory in the selection of information communicated to each group. If one accepts the principle that the interests and objectives of participants in Europe's industrial democracy must somehow be harmonized, what more logical place to start than the annual corporate report?

Management tends to overestimate the sophistication of the stockholder and underestimate that of the worker. As we have mentioned elsewhere, a strong case can be made for the production of the basic company annual report fulfilling the common information needs of stockholder, worker, civil servant, politician, journalist, environmentalist and consumer (detailing company activities and achievements, key data on economic and social performance, future prospects, etc.). This would be accompanied by separate supplements giving greater detail on issues of interest to workers, banks and stockholders and special interest groups of particular relevance to individual companies.

There are two vehicles of communication that management can use to cut across the more established channels of communication with workers, and thus avoid the inherent impersonality of published media. One is closed-circuit and video television, and the other is the annual meeting for employee representatives.

An increasing number of companies are using the annual meeting forum, most usually associated with stockholders, to communicate directly with the lower levels of company management and employee representatives. Usually the format of the meeting is similar to that of the stockholders' meeting (except that it tends to be very much better attended). It is an opportunity for management to explain not just the company's historical performance, but also its opportunities, objectives and broad strategies for the future. It also gives top management an opportunity to hear and discuss first-hand the concerns of its workers, especially in those companies that lack other effective channels of internal communication through works councils, etc.

The use of closed-circuit and video recorded television for communication with employees can be most effective, if also very expensive. It enables management to reach a very large audience on a much more personal and immediate basis than employee newspapers and similar media. But the medium of television is such that it will exaggerate an executive's weaknesses as effectively as it can project his strengths of personality and authority. It is a medium requiring more than just personal sincerity. The basic skills and techniques required to exploit its potential in the controlled context of communicating with employees are easily learned, however.

The importance of internal communication is well recognized by the 400 or so chief executives whose opinions we surveyed. Only a few said that their top and middle management did not currently receive company information on a regular basis. While, disturbingly, one in five said this also applied to their non-management employees, much less than one in ten of those surveyed felt industry need not communicate with them on a regular basis.

Recognition of the need to communicate, however, does not in itself ensure effective communication. With employees, perhaps more than with any other group, ineffective communication is not just wasteful. It is a potential hazard to the successful day-to-day operation of an enterprise in Europe, and strikes at the very core of business survival.

7

Teachers and Students

Industry should, in defence of its own future, attempt to become more integrated in the process of education. The present gap between business enterprise and the institutions that mould the attitudes and aspirations of tomorrow's workers and managers is too large to ignore. Education, in the context of Europe's industrial democracy, is far too important to be left to the teachers.

With very few exceptions, teachers and students have been largely ignored by industry in Europe. The result is that in most countries students more often prefer to choose an academic or civil service career. By largely ignoring the process of education, presumably in the belief that young people are factors of society that need little consideration until they are old enough to work, industry must now wrestle with a whole generation of individuals whose personal objectives differ sharply from those of their parents.

Since World War II, education has undergone a revolution across Europe. Prewar concepts of discipline, competition and a fairly universal respect for authority have largely passed into folklore. They have been replaced by a new set of values. On average throughout Europe today's young men and women have had more than twice as much school education as workers now approaching retirement, and a kind of education that has encouraged them to question the *status quo* almost as a matter of course.

All of this has been a generation or more in the making, and industry has done little to either influence or accept the process. Mostly, it has complained about what has come out the other end.

In recent years senior industrialists and even socialist politicians in Europe (including at least one prime minister) have openly questioned the validity of national education policies. In Britain a major government inquiry and public debate is under way to examine how educational policy can be changed to produce people better fitted for the practical realities of life, and the needs of society and industry. As Britain's minister for education (Mrs Shirley Williams) said at the end of 1976 when the issue opened up for public debate: 'There is always endless pressure for further inquiries in the education world. Sometimes, it seems, we should take a little action.'

A recommendation for industry as well, perhaps?

The very same week Lord Ryder, chairman of Britain's National Enterprise Board, said:

> Somehow we need to convince intelligent young people entering the job market that industry, and line management in particular, is not a dirty word and that the creation of wealth, of national wealth, is just as personally satisfying and as socially useful as being a teacher, social worker or government official.

Businessmen in Europe will argue that the basic system of education today is preparing young people for a world that does not exist. Most teachers, on the other hand, will not accept any suggestion that their function is to equip young men and women with ambitions no broader then 'the producer role' as seen by industry. Teaching, like journalism, attracts the politically active mind. It must be no surprise therefore if teachers are biased by sincerely held political and social views that are at odds with the traditions and current realities of business enterprise.

There are three areas of the education world that require separate consideration by business and industry in Europe: the business schools and university departments offering business-related courses, universities in general, and the secondary level of pre-university school education. While priority of effort is largely directed at the first area, the other two must not be ignored. The areas of university education that are not directly related to industry are important to the general climate for business enterprise, and a great many university students not following a business-related course will join industry or could be encouraged to do so. The secondary level of school education is important because it establishes personal and career aspirations that condition attitudes to work, for those that go straight into the job market, and the choice of options available to those who go on to university.

At the level of pre-university education the problem is chiefly one of the relevance of the expectations and demands instilled in youth. This problem is wholly a postwar phenomenon, partly because there is no real history of popular education much beyond the basic elements of literacy and numeracy (and even this is not true of some European countries before the second quarter of this century). Industry's only effective contribution to this dramatic expansion of popular education has been to provide the national wealth that has made it possible. It is, perhaps, a perverse sense of justice that has made the traditional values of industrial enterprise a chief casualty of the process.

At the university level the problem is not so much the number of students following business-related courses (though this is an issue in a few countries), it is more the relevance of those courses to the needs of industry. This problem is well recognized by students following a business-related course. This group of students is represented world-wide by AIESEC (the international association of students in economics and management). AIESEC has over 20,000 members in 350 universities in fifty-five countries and the theme of the Association's work in 1977 and 1978 is 'Business Education in the 1980s'. Exclusively for this book, the International AIESEC Secretariat carried out a survey among its national presidents in Europe and America, most of whom are graduates and full-time officers, or in their final year of study.

STUDENT VIEWS OF INDUSTRY

The survey was conducted at the beginning of 1977. It revealed some striking facts about what students know about industry and its needs when they have to decide what university course to follow, the relevance of management courses at university level, and where students think the blame and solution lies.

In Europe a student has to decide what type of course he or she will follow at university on average at the age of eighteen, ranging from seventeen in some countries to nineteen and twenty in others. In some countries, the field of choice is narrowed by an earlier process of specialization resulting from examination at the age of fifteen. At the time of selecting a university course the vast majority of students have little or no practical understanding of business and industry. What small understanding they do have tends to be based on textbooks, newspapers and business magazines (and school career advisers, who seldom have experience in industry or much practical contact with business). The only students to have any first-hand experience of industry at this point are those whose families own a business or those who take holiday jobs in industry (this is particularly popular in Scandinavia). Actual knowledge of industry improves a little in some countries among students following a business-related course. It is only in the United States, however, that such students tend to have a great deal of contact with industry. And while in the United States students *not* following a business-related course have some contact with industry, in Europe contact ranges from 'a little' to 'none at all'.

The AIESEC student leaders we surveyed think the blame for this is fairly evenly split between business, universities and the students themselves – with students being marginally less responsible than business, and universities being somewhat more responsible.

When the student leaders were asked to what extent the system of education in their country was geared to the needs of business and industry, *as seen by the businessman,* virtually all of them replied 'a little' or 'not at all'. They noted that there was considerable criticism by business and industry in most European countries of the quality of students completing a business-related course. They said that business students felt this situation called much more for a change in university courses than a change in the policy and practice of business and industry (by a factor of 2 : 1). But comments from the student leaders clearly indicated that they felt business should take the initiative for change. The following are some of the comments that emerged on this point.

1. 'Industry should push for joint representation on university boards that set college courses. Businessmen should do more to encourage links between themselves and academics, and be more willing to come and speak to students.'

2. 'Develop a more positive attitude to students, especially those studying business and economics. Industry must be presented more widely and effectively on campus as a good career choice.'

3. 'Industry must try to a greater extent to influence teaching at universities by sending personnel to speak about the practical side of business life – we seem to learn too much about the theory of it.'

4. 'Industry should be more open to theories coming from the universities, to give universities a greater chance to test their work in

companies. Students should have more opportunities to work and get experience in companies during studies.'

5. 'Businessmen should try to get more influence at Ministry level, work more intensively with universities in providing practical case material, participate in seminars arranged by schools and student organizations, and encourage their own employees to be active members of post-graduate associations.'

6. 'Industry must be more active in education – helping with business games and lending out their own educational programmes. It must take more interest in forming educational systems. There must be a two-way flow of information between industry, students and teachers.'

The comments of national AIESEC presidents on what they thought the objectives of companies in their countries are today, and what they felt they should be, were encouraging – even accepting that these student leaders are by definition more in tune with business than are students in general.

Survival, profit and growth were the words most commonly used to describe today's business objectives. There was some acknowledgement in a few countries of objectives related to the best interests of employees, and the fact that product quality and satisfying consumer needs were contributing factors to survival.

Survival, profit and growth were also central factors in what those surveyed felt a company's objectives should be. However, an overwhelming majority felt these objectives should be broadened. Comments such as the following were typical.

1. 'Companies must realize they play a social role. To make profit must be an objective, but not the only one.'

2. 'To survive and maximize profit, but taking into consideration the company's employment role, and plan for more than just survival.'

3. 'To give all parties interested [employed] in the company a reasonable possibility to meet their personal expectations.'

4. 'To regard more the company's responsibility towards the whole community, the social role.'

Encouraging though this aspect of the AIESEC survey may be to business management (since those surveyed represent the new generation of students that are actually planning to make a career of industry), other findings of the survey are most disturbing. The full-time officials that run AIESEC's international secretariat feel that the following four factors are of special and urgent concern for industry in Europe:

1. the very low level of knowledge and understanding that students have of business and industry when they have to decide on the type of university course to follow;
2. the lack of contact between business and even those students that are following a business-related course;
3. the generally poor contact between business and the teaching staffs of universities;
4. the low level of practical relevance of most university courses to the needs of business and industry.

The AIESEC staff feel that other problems also result from the lack of co-operation between business and the education world. For example, quite apart from the lack of relevance to industry's needs of current university courses, the present system provides a disturbing imbalance of graduate skills. In one period of time universities will produce twice as many engineers as industry can use and too few economists; five years later the situation is reversed – all because neither students nor universities yet have sufficient data to determine industry's future needs, even in very broad terms.

Companies that already have a relationship with universities, beyond the annual recruiting drive, tend to be in specialized research-based industries like chemicals and computers. The relationship tends as a result to be heavily biased towards the science and research departments. Some of the largest American companies have full-time staff that specialize in university relations, but very few companies in Europe have gone this far yet. For the most part, European companies that have strong internal training programmes tend to have links with one or two business schools and universities; but these are usually informal, *ad hoc* in character, and primarily dependent on the contacts and enthusiasm of the company's training department.

Student leaders feel that much more initiative and action must come from industry for at least two reasons: students have insufficient influence on their own, and the teaching faculty have insufficient incentive to reform the present system. Indeed, the very idea of industry becoming involved directly in the formulation of university courses and the teaching process profoundly disturbs a large number of teachers. They are concerned that it would challenge their current prerogatives and possibly push cherished academic theory into the wilting spotlight of practical experience. This is less true, perhaps, of the business schools, but it is certainly true of many university departments offering courses that are not directly related to business enterprise, such as philosophy and political science.

The desire of academics to retain complete freedom from commerce presents the biggest obstacle to direct involvement of industry in 'their territory' – that, coupled with the scepticism with which each regards the other's contribution to society, and their entirely different frames of reference. To the businessman, the academic is over-read and under-experienced, over-dependent on theory, and cosseted in an artificial environment. To the academic, the businessman is crassly and personally commercial, too narrow in his vision, and reluctant to change established patterns. The student is left unhappily in the middle, like the child of an unstable marriage. They know that both 'parents' have a valid point of view and believe that something must be done to bring them together for the common good of all three. The academic probably has more at risk, and least to gain, from a closer relationship with industry. This is why initiative for change must come from the latter.

SECONDARY SCHOOL NEEDS

At the secondary level of school education, industry's lack of involvement in education takes on a new and worrying significance in the context of worker participation and Europe's emerging brand of industrial democracy. In addition to learning the basics of numeracy and literacy, children are being indoctrinated with value judgements that are frequently at odds with today's industrial realities. As a result, school-leavers enter industry with attitudes and expectations that will not, and in many cases can not, be met.

Here again, teachers (with the exception of those in some private schools) will claim that it is not their job to produce individuals who will fit neatly and quietly into the requirements of today's industrial structure. They see their role as providing young people with skills and attitudes that will broaden their aspirations for life as a whole, beyond that part of it that must be spent earning a living. While this is a defensible position, the political orientation, lack of industrial experience and general attitude of most teachers at this level to business enterprise means that a dialogue between the two is long overdue. The lack of understanding, and very often respect, that each has for the other is rooted in part at least in ignorance of each other's aspirations and contributions to society.

Industry must also strive to achieve a more direct relationship with pupils at the secondary level of school education. It must participate in discussions on industry's impact on society, the environment, and the economic wellbeing of a community. The relationship between industry and both teachers and pupils at the secondary school level is most relevant and most practical at the local level. It is most relevant because the majority of pupils will be potential employees for local industry, and most practical because the relationship is more easily managed 'on the spot'.

Apart from the business school, the information needs and expectations of teachers and students are sporadic and *ad hoc*. For example, industry is occasionally asked to arrange factory visits for school groups. Often these requests are denied, and even when they are accepted they are frequently handled poorly. Too often industry tries to impress such groups with its machinery and processes, giving scant attention to the people involved. It is hardly surprising that these visitors leave the factory with an uninspired concept of 'man serving the machine', and a jaundiced view of industry as a career choice. Industry is also expected to provide information both to teachers wanting data to prove or disprove a particular point and to students working on a research project or thesis. Even this limited expectation is not met by most companies because the effort involved in supplying the data exceeds any likely immediate return. Further, there is some scepticism as to how the information will actually be interpreted. Such requests are usually addressed to the managing director and end up at a low level in the personnel or public relations department where they are overwhelmed and discarded by the priorities of the day. This is inevitable if there is no established method for handling such requests.

Not only should industry make every effort to meet these meagre demands; but it should, in defence of its own future, attempt to become more interested in the process of education. The present gap between business enterprise and the institutions that mould the attitudes and aspirations of tomorrow's workers and managers is too large to ignore. Education, in the context of Europe's industrial democracy, is far too important to be left to teachers.

ACTION FROM INDUSTRY

Other demands on industrial enterprise come from such groups as AIESEC. As we noted earlier, it has many concerns about the relationship at the moment and the ability of business education to meet the practical needs of industry. AIESEC sponsors student exchange programmes (involving some 4,000 students each year), promotes student internships in industry during their studies, and runs seminars to promote greater mutual understanding between business students, teachers and industry. There are many other organizations with similar ambitions, at local, national and international levels. None complain of an over-enthusiastic response from industry.

Among the actions that the larger companies should consider at national and international levels are:

1. the appointment of a full or part-time manager to liaise with the education world;

2. the development of national/international strategy and action programme for relating with business schools and universities at teaching faculty and student levels. This would necessarily involve evaluation of existing relationships, and assessment of needed relationships to:

   (a) promote the company's interests and ensure it has the pick of available graduates;

   (b) improve the relevance of business-related courses and their practical content;

   (c) increase the understanding of the education world of the practical aspirations and needs of business enterprise;

   (d) improve the company's understanding of the academic viewpoint on such issues as business ethics, social and economic performance, and fundamental business objectives.

In addition to being relevant objectives for larger companies operating in Europe, the last three are especially (perhaps more) appropriate for action by industry federations and associations. It will require deliberate pressure, however, from individual member companies for this to happen.

Additionally, *all* companies with any potential impact in a community should consider:

1. assigning one senior executive to liaise part-time at local plant level with local educational institutions (secondary schools, technical schools and colleges, etc.) at both teaching and pupil levels;

2. developing a local programme to:

   (a) promote the company's interests and ensure it has the pick of school-leavers;

   (b) improve the reputation of industry as a productive and satisfying field of employment;

   (c) improve the practical understanding of teachers of the favourable social and economic impact of industry at local community level;

   (d) improve the company's understanding of the broader objectives of education, especially at the secondary level.

While these are appropriate activities for all companies in a community, there is scope here too for a stronger role to be played by local business clubs, chambers of commerce, etc. At the very least these clubs provide a forum where business managers can discuss the problem and agree on a strategy for joint or separate action. It would represent a worthwhile investment in the future success and survival of business enterprise.

8

Special Interest Groups

The European environment and consumer protection movements are sceptical of Nader-style tactics. However, once Europe's economic recession is over, leaving public and political opinion much more receptive to such pressures, both movements will be marching with a more determined step to a much louder tune.

Industry on both sides of the Atlantic has to contend with a great number of special interest groups. These include organizations, both official and self-appointed, that seek to represent the interests of specific segments of society or specific viewpoints. There are hundreds. They range from 'women's lib' organizations and those representing minority race and religious groups to more broadly based organizations representing consumers and the environmental protection movement.

Apart from sharing the same basic objective – to protect or extend the rights of the special interests they represent – their most common denominator is their diversity; not just diversity of interest, but diversity of motivation, funding, organizational strength, and methods of achieving their objectives.

Organizations representing racial or religious groups as well as the women's movement have frequently sought the help of industry directly in pursuit of their objectives in Europe. Those representing Germany's guest-workers and their families and Britain's coloured population are among them.

But the two groups that are most common to industry as a whole in Europe, and that represent a universal challenge, are those representing consumers and the environmental protection movement. They represent a challenge that appears to be well recognized by top management. Our research among chief executives in Europe indicates that both organizations were at the bottom of a list of some twenty groups of 'key publics' with which industrial management communicates on a regular basis today. However, when asked which publics management *should* communicate with, both groups moved up sharply. Only 13 per cent of the chief executives questioned said they communicated regularly with consumer organizations and 15 per cent with environmental groups; 55 per cent said industry *should* communicate on a regular basis with consumer groups and 46 per cent with environmental organizations.

We shall concentrate on these two groups in this chapter. We shall examine some of the key characteristics of each and the essential differences that separate them, and we shall discuss industry's response to their claims and activities.

In Europe these groups have one curious factor in common. While their objectives (in so far as they relate to industry) call for a change in company standards and policy, neither seeks a relationship or dialogue with industrial management. There are exceptions to this in some countries; but this general rule applies to more than 90 per cent of both groups. There are three primary reasons for this.

1. Both groups feel their credibility and assumed honest impartiality would be tainted if they were seen to be talking with industry. This is especially true of consumer groups, because most of these in Europe concentrate on 'comparative testing' of products and services. In this area provable impartiality is essential.

2. Neither group has much confidence in a voluntary responsiveness by industry. Both believe that significant change will result only from legislation.

3. With few exceptions the organizations in both groups operate with very limited financial resources and staff. Necessity therefore forces them to focus attention on a few priority activities, with the best chances of success.

There is, however, a marked difference between the way in which these groups pursue their objectives. There is a significant difference, too, between the conduct of both in Europe and the United States.

As with organizations representing the rights of women and minority ethnic groups, consumer and environmental protection organizations in the United States tend to be much more aggressively action-oriented than their European counterparts. The highly successful activity of Ralph Nader and the 'Nader Raiders' in the United States is but one example. Quite apart from any judgement one may make about the more aggressive character of the nation itself and its urgent pursuit of fashionable causes, there is one other fundamental reason for this difference in policy and style: the use of litigation. Whereas taking an individual or company to court is often the concluding phase of a disagreement in Europe, legal action is a priority weapon in the United States. Argument in open court is an effective method of arousing public awareness and winning results. The European approach has been different.

CONSUMER ASSOCIATIONS

To begin with, few consumer associations in Europe regard themselves as a part of a 'movement'. While some were started with government funding, almost all began as an information service for private subscribers, based on entirely independent research and comparative testing of products and services. The information was, and still is, conveyed to subscribers through publications like *Which?* in Britain, *Que choisir?* and *50 millions de Consommateurs* in France and *Test Achats* in Belgium. Almost all consumer associations in Europe were founded in the late 1950s and early 1960s, several decades after similar organizations were established in the United States.

The primary role of most consumer associations in Europe was, therefore, to provide a select group of subscribers with an advantage over other consumers. Very little effort was made in the early days to spread this knowledge to a wider audience, and to promote the interests of consumers at large. Indeed, there still remain powerful forces within many of the consumer associations in Europe against an extension of their activities and a change in their essentially passive style.

But changes have taken place, and there can be little doubt that more dramatic changes are in store for the next decade.

Take Britain's Consumer Association as an example. It is one of the oldest in Europe, and has become one of the richest too by providing a reliable independent information service to private subscribers. Its reputation for thoroughness and impartiality remains largely unchallenged and is a cherished asset. Despite some internal resistance, its scope of operation has enlarged over the past decade from dealing with the comparative testing of goods to cover commercial, health and welfare services, and even taxation. The outmoded definition of 'consumer' has thus been broadened to encompass other citizen rights. At the same time the organization has been conscious of the limits of its historical impact – a limitation due to its almost exclusive appeal to middle-class subscribers, and to its reliance for effect simply upon the provision of well researched fact. It developed something of a guilty conscience about the limit of its appeal, and a sense of frustration at the limit of its effect.

Both factors have tended to drive the organization into a more active role in championing broader principles of consumer protection and lobbying for improved legislation. It has become more expert in identifying issues of potential public anxiety, and at helping to create public awareness. Examples in recent years include the information content of product labels, the safety of domestic electrical appliances and the activities of mortgage bankers and package-tour holiday operators.

This general trend is apparent in other countries too. Indeed, there are consumer associations in France and Belgium that have become extremely active as pressure groups. They have tackled with considerable aggression such issues as the mercury level in fish and the related concern over the effects of sea pollution on the condition of holiday beaches.

'The move towards a more aggressive role for consumer associations in lobbying for improved consumer protection is a logical and probably inevitable development,' says Miss Eirlys Roberts, director of the European Bureau of Consumer Unions:

> Experience has taught us all that if you believe something needs to be changed, merely making information available is not enough. Ensuring the information is in the hands of and understood by those who can effect a change is a necessity. Inevitably this calls for political lobbying to ensure stricter standards through legislation.

Inevitably? Certainly the historical experience of consumer associations leads to this conclusion. Without legislative pressure, or the threat of it, it is difficult to think that there would have been much positive change in the advertising practices of tobacco and pharmaceutical firms, the wording and application of some manufacturers' guarantees, and even safety standards of children's toys and clothes.

Already, consumer associations in Europe are encouraged by their recent successes in the more active forms of consumer advocacy. The traditional conservatism of most consumer organizations, and their historical reluctance to forsake their scientific cocoon for a more political role, will continue to have one foot on the brake; but a new breed of consumer advocate already has a foot on the accelerator. Few believe that a European Ralph Nader will emerge; but industry can expect a build-up of political pressure from consumer associations in most countries of Europe.

ENVIRONMENTALIST MOVEMENTS

The environmental protection movement, by contrast, learned the value of political pressure at a very early stage of its development in Europe. It has been the movement's chief weapon, and at the centre of virtually all of its many successes. The anti-nuclear lobby across Europe is a splendid example. While this has sometimes been accompanied and overshadowed by violent protest action, as in Germany, it has been the central weapon of most national anti-nuclear campaigns organized by environmental protection groups. Section Four of this book contains a case-study on the highly successful government relations and communication programme carried out by the Dutch Reflection Group on Energy Policy.

Environmental protection is essentially a grass-roots movement. In Europe there are about 3,000 permanent organizations at local, regional and national levels. The local and regional organizations tend to be privately funded and operated by part-time volunteers, whereas many of the national organizations receive government grants. In addition, there are thousands of other *ad hoc* groups formed to solve one particular local environmental problem. This might be the preservation of a building, preventing the construction of a motorway or factory, cleaning up an oil-fouled beach or eye-sore in the countryside. They tend to last as long as the problem exists, and are then disbanded.

The environment and its protection mean different things to different people, of course. A farmer will have a different concept of the environment than an industrial worker; an ornithologist will have a different view than someone interested in the preservation of old buildings. Much of the environmental protection movement is concerned with issues that involve industry only peripherally: the siting of a new airport, the reconstruction of a town centre or the extension of a motorway. But much of the movement is also wholly concerned with issues that are directly related to industrial activity: pollution from industrial waste, the hazards of new technologies, depletion of the world's natural resources for industrial production, the location and design of new factories.

'Environmental protection has all the characteristics of a political movement,' according to Mr Hubert David, director of the European Environmental Bureau:

It consists of people believing in an ideology and dealing with issues that are often very local and not very tangible. The emphasis of the movement is much more on prevention than cure. With the right kind of pressure it is much easier to prevent the building of a motor-way or nuclear power plant than to have it torn down after it is built.

The emphasis on prevention rather than cure is another factor that distinguishes the environmental protection movement from consumer organizations. Indeed, the environmental movement has few successes to its credit in curing environmental problems after they have been created. This is largely because the more significant problems are extremely costly to cure and it is frequently difficult to determine where the bill should be sent.

Because of its diversity, and the very local nature of many of the issues it deals with, the environmental protection movement tends to have a much broader popular base than the largely middle-class base of the consumer organizations. Because of its need for often quite complex scientific data, the environmental protection movement has very close ties with the science and research departments of European universities – a milieu that tends to give the movement an anti-industry bias. Indeed, in some countries the movement has staunchly and openly anarchistic tendencies.

All of these factors divide the two groups we have examined briefly in this chapter. It is perhaps because of these differences in orientation and style that they seldom work together on common problems. The case of sea pollution resulting in contaminated fish and polluted beaches that we described earlier is just one example.

PREPARATION FOR THE FUTURE

Industry can expect a change in this in the future, however, as the consumer organizations become more militant and action-oriented. The synergy created by both movements working on the same problem will certainly shift the balance and power of their influence over legislation affecting the conduct of industry.

Industry also faces the prospect of a much better co-ordinated attack at the international level in both consumer and environmental areas. Both groups have become much better organized at the European level in recent years. There are also signs of increasing co-ordination on a world-wide basis – and not only through such institutions as the United Nations and OECD. The environmental protection movement has long recognized that one of its chief handicaps is the cost of implementing its proposals, and the effect of that cost on the competitiveness of an industry in one country in the context of international trade. In the past an industry in one country has always pleaded that the cost of reducing its polluting waste drastically would push overall production costs up so far it would be driven out of business by industries in other countries that have less strict standards. This argument has an economic logic. While a great deal of work is being done at the moment to solve this issue at government level, fresh impetus is also coming now from other institutions – for example, some of the giant trusts and foundations in the United States.

A recent example of this was concern about pollution of the river Rhine. Environmentalists in Europe had been trying for some time to organize a conference attended by government officials and its own members from all the five countries through which the river (known as 'the sewer of Europe') and its tributaries flow. The idea was eventually pursued by one of the national governments; but it was only with financial and other help from a major US foundation that the meeting had become a practical reality.

Consumer and environmental protection are issues that European industry has had to contend with at a much lower level of pressure than industry in the United States. Organizations to protect and promote the interests of both groups have been slower to form, more reluctant and less able through lack of funds to pursue their objectives with the same level of urgency and drama as those in the United States. The European environment and consumer protection movements are sceptical of Nader-style tactics. However, once Europe's economic recession is over, leaving public and political opinion much more receptive to such pressures, both movements will be marching with a more determined step to a much louder tune.

Industrial management would be wise therefore to decide in advance how it plans to tackle this increased challenge. A key dilemma is the almost total cynicism and mistrust that characterizes the attitudes of both groups towards industry, and their resulting reluctance to engage in almost any form of dialogue. A state of impasse currently exists. Neither group believes industry is sufficiently responsive to indulge in effective self-regulation and sees legislation as the only solution. So far as industrial management is concerned, both these groups include ill-informed do-gooders who have little understanding of the complexities and limits of industrial production. (In fact, many within both groups readily admit to this. They justify it by asserting that ignorance is a price they must pay to keep industry at arm's length.)

However, many of the consumer associations are beginning to see the need of dialogue with industry in meeting their objectives of higher standards of consumer protection. Indeed, some already have a relationship through government-sponsored consumer councils. With government present as a referee, they feel more comfortable about the continued protection of their cherished integrity.

Of course, it would be quite wrong to suggest that industry has done nothing to respond to the more legitimate objectives of consumer and environmental protectionists. Some companies have made a considerable effort to react with enlightened responsibility. It is not enough, however, for some to lead and only a few to follow – with the bulk of industry fighting a rear-guard battle against the forces of legitimate change.

> If industry were to spend on anticipating and preventing environmental conflicts and on the creation of positive public dialogue and education only a portion of what it now spends on adversary proceedings, the prospects for achieving greater harmony between the economic and environmental aspects of growth would be vastly enhanced – and I submit that both the environment and the economy would be better off.

So said Mr Maurice Strong, chairman of the giant Petro-Canada, on receiving the Pahlavi International Environment Prize in 1976. He went on to say:

> What is needed at this point is a means of mobilizing the resources of individual citizens, private organizations and corporations, to support the kind of programmes of public education, positive dialogue, citizen action, innovation and experimentation which can supplement and complement the role of governments and official organizations.

In deciding whether and how to strengthen its policy towards environmental and consumer protection groups European industry should accept two premises.

1. There will be increasing public and political concern on consumer and environmental issues over the next decade (owing in part at least to the improved effectiveness of environmental and consumer protection movements).

2. Some measure of self-regulation will be necessary to avoid retaliatory and punitive legislation. However, the only practical method of

improving general standards of consumer and environmental protection is sensible, internationally co-ordinated legislation.

The promotion of informed public debate, and improved dialogue between industry, pressure groups and legislators, must be clear priorities for industrial management in Europe on these issues. Breaking down the reluctance of pressure group leaders to talk with industry is a problem. But perhaps it is not a completely insoluble one. A first step would be to improve the flow of information from industry to consumer and environmental protection organizations, even if there is little return flow at first. At the very least this would help the more sincere elements in these organizations, the bulk of them, to avoid making silly mistakes in pronouncing judgement on the behaviour of industry. Whereas it will doubtless prove extremely difficult for individual companies to form a productive relationship with these organizations, it would be considerably easier and more practical for industry and trade associations; they represent the interests of industry as a whole, or at least large segments of it, and are once removed from the perceived source of the problem. They could play a much more effective role as an intermediary and channel of communication.

At the same time, however, industry must improve its contact with those responsible for the drafting of legislation and regulation to balance the information and ideas flowing from the various pressure groups. Government in most of Europe has established a mechanism for this through such institutions as consumer councils and environmental consultative groups. However, industry has not always ensured that its best talent represents it in these bodies. Too often, industry's case is poorly made by inexpert representatives.

Improved public debate must also be an essential element in a more purposeful response by industry to consumer and environmental issues. This is needed not only because the public is affected by the consequences of industry's behaviour; but because the quality of legislation will be conditioned by the strength and direction of public opinion.

Both environmental and consumer protection groups in Europe are girding their loins for a more determined pursuit of their objectives, once the economic conditions improve and make this politically practical. Industry therefore has a choice. It can acknowledge this inevitability and develop a pre-emptive strategy to help solve the issues involved through constructive long-term planning and encouraging a better informed climate of opinion; alternatively, it can plead the pressure of other priorities today, and wait till it sees 'the whites of their eyes' to engage ill-prepared in the crisis of conflict.

9

The Press

There are many different kinds of journalists – an extraordinary range in terms of technical competence, objectivity and sincerity. The range is probably almost as wide as it is in senior management in industry. It is both unwise and unfair, therefore, for businessmen to expect any universal norm to exist in the press any more than it does in their own area of activity.

Our survey of European chief executives confirmed the importance most companies attach to communicating with the media. Of more than 400 chief executives questioned, 61 per cent said that their companies maintain active press relations and 81 per cent said that they think press relations are important for companies in general. Indeed, the survey concluded that chief executives feel the most important single method of communicating company information is through the press. But before taking a look at the information needs and expectations of the press it is necessary to understand something of its structure in Europe and the kind of men and women who fill its pages and broadcast programmes.

Published media are usually a combination of three separate characteristics. They are:

1. national, regional or local;
2. daily, weekly or monthly;
3. popular, serious or specialist.

The almost total absence of European news media, that is to say media with a Europe-wide orientation and readership (possible exceptions include the *International Herald Tribune* and *Vision)*, is only partly a result of the absence of a common language and an increase in coverage of European affairs in national media. It is more a reflection of the disunity and diversity that persists within the Continent. European media that were started in the 1960s to catch on to the coat-tails of the European dream have either died or are struggling for survival.

There are very great differences in the structure, orientation and sophistication of the press from country to country in Europe. For instance, the national daily press is an especially strong factor in Britain. Indeed, no other country has a national press that is anything like as strong in numbers, readership or influence as that of Britain. France has a national daily press, but with a disproportionately large distribution in (and orientation towards) the nation's capital. Italy, likewise, has a few so-called national newspapers, but again their focus tends to be very regional. In Germany, because of the political structure imposed on the country after World War II, there are almost no national daily newspapers. For different reasons Spain has virtually no truly national daily press, either. In fact, in Germany, France, Italy, Spain and Scandinavia the regional press dominates the daily media scene along with television and radio.

While Britain, uniquely, has a strong and relatively thriving Sunday newspaper industry, all four major industrial nations of Europe (Germany, France, Britain and Italy) are well served by nationally distributed weekly and monthly magazines. This holds true for the political and business sectors as well as general news and special interest areas.

Television is of course the new technology of mass communication. It now fills several times over the role that radio played in mass communication up to two or three decades ago in most countries (though much less than this in some countries like Portugal, Greece and Norway). Most countries have national broadcasting networks, with provision for some regional programmes – the big exception again being Germany which has only regional networks.

Television can be a frightening medium to work with. This is especially true for a businessman in a crisis, which is usually the only situation in which most are likely to have any direct contact with it. Television has dramatic impact. Anyone who is ever likely to become involved with the medium should go on one of the many courses available to train senior industrial management in how to 'perform' to best effect. It is no place for amateurs. While this is much less true of radio, the same basic principles apply.

The advent of television has had some impact on the structure and role of the published media too, but nothing like the impact of straightforward economic factors. Throughout most of Europe the last two decades have seen a reduction especially in the number of newspapers, and to a lesser extent of magazines. The pressure of economic factors like wage inflation and the cost of both raw materials and distribution have been compounded by technological advances in printing equipment that have greatly reduced the industry's manpower requirements. The strength of the print unions, especially in Britain and France, have been such that chronic over-manning has resulted. No businessman needs to be told about the economic havoc this leads to if it is allowed to persist for long. In fact, the newspaper industry is frequently held by business journalists themselves (and not always in private) to be a good example of bad management and even worse labour relations. This may of course contribute towards the frequently jaundiced eye with which they view the rest of industry.

POLITICAL AND PERSONAL BIAS

The press in Germany and Britain is probably the most objective and credible in Europe. The media in France is heavily politicized and much of that in Italy is owned by and represents vested interest. Indeed, the press in Italy and Spain, not to mention countries like Portugal, is a relatively new phenomenon of mass communication for the simple reason that universal literacy has come to these countries only comparatively recently. Censorship, too, crippled the press in Spain and Portugal until the dramatic political changes of very recent history. Whereas economic factors have forced considerable rationalization of the press in most of Europe, the political emancipation of these two countries has made the press one of their biggest single growth industries. The number of serious newspapers and magazines in Spain has doubled since the death of General Franco, and the readership of some (while still tiny compared to those of Germany, Britain and France) has multiplied ten-fold.

The quality and seriousness of the media, and the depth of its coverage of social, economic and political events, have increased at about the same pace as the educational and political sophistication of the population groups they seek to serve. A good case can be made to support the thesis that the press has played a major role in increasing the expectations if not altogether the sophistication of their readers. Certainly the political orientation of the media, or perhaps more accurately of the journalist, has been a key factor in the almost universal drift of Europe to the political Left. Journalism attracts the politically active. These days the views expressed by most of the more influential media in Europe reflect less and less the views of their proprietors. The only exceptions to this are tightly run empires like that of Axel Springer in Germany. But whereas journalists may now be more independent of their employers, they do not necessarily as a result possess greater objectivity in reporting and commenting on events of the day. It is merely perhaps that their 'control' has shifted into a political rather than a commercial camp. Some journalists are more concerned, too, with the opinions of other journalists than with those of other readers.

More and more in Europe these days, possession of a union card is as essential a part of a journalist's equipment as pencil and notebook. Increasingly, too, senior editorial appointments in the media, including that of editor, rest as much with the journalists as management. Indeed, there are recent precedents for the change of ownership of a newspaper or magazine resting largely on the expressed preference of the editorial staff. Many journalists therefore have a close working experience of and affinity with concepts like worker participation, and most of those journalists who have no such experience yet seem to crave for it. It is after all an intriguing prospect for any politically agile mind.

The best and most reliable journalists do not necessarily write for the more serious and traditionally best respected media. It is as incorrect to assume that they do as it is to assume there is a universally high calibre of manager in the biggest and most financially successful corporations. But a manager has a significant advantage over a journalist in that the latter's work is much more public. The journalist cannot, unlike the manager, spend an entire career with professional inadequacies and incompetence concealed from general view. Unfortunately, however, a highly competent businessman can be represented as an incompetent buffoon by a journalist who is either careless or less than honest himself. Indeed, sloppy or deliberately mischievous reporting is facilitated in some European countries by very liberal laws of libel.

There is a safeguard in most of these countries, however, which many companies seem reluctant to use: a legal right of reply. If a newspaper or magazine publishes an error, deliberately or not, it is legally obliged in much of Europe to publish a correction if requested to do so. Invoking this right does not necessarily lose friends in the press if the situation is handled diplomatically and if the original error has caused real damage or embarrassment. Newspapers, like people, do not like to admit to having made a mistake; but proper use of the right to reply can increase the level of mutual respect.

Journalists play a unique role in communication in that they both express their own views and act as a channel for the expression of other people's opinions. It is a neat balancing act; but it is a very rare journalist indeed who does not permit his own opinions to filter, however subconsciously, the expression of views he or she does not personally support. Journalists are human, after all.

But aside from these personal preconditions and limitations, there are more practical and more tangible factors governing the information needs and expectations of the press.

INFORMATION NEEDS

In the first place the press has very few regular information needs and expectations so far as most companies are concerned. Most journalists, when asked, will say their information requirements from any individual company are sporadic and *ad hoc*. They neither need nor encourage a steady flow. They are already swamped daily with extraneous information, irrelevant press releases and pictures that find their way into the waste basket practically as a matter of course. They will explain that news, which is by definition a departure from the norm and the prime commodity in which they deal, is rarely created by public relations departments. News occurs, or is the result of a combination of circumstances. But when this industrial chemistry produces an event worth reporting, the information needs of the press are considerable and immediate.

Second, there is the category of media. The information needs of a television news programme or popular national daily newspaper will be far removed from the expectations of a local weekly paper. So too will be those of the industrial editor of a 'serious' national daily.

Let us take a factory strike to illustrate the point. The television news programme and popular national daily will want a few key facts like how many people are involved, what started it all and so forth. They will want a simple quote from management, preferably one that contradicts any statement from the strikers. The story will have added news value if the effect of the strike is the loss of a big export order, if they can get interviews with and pictures of the strike leaders, or if there is some personal hard-luck story involved.

The local newspaper probably has most of the salient information already from non-management and even non-company sources. It will want a lot more names of local people involved, however, and will want to assess the impact of the strike on the local community and other businesses in the area.

The industrial editor of the 'serious' national daily will want to have a much broader perspective of the economic and social implications of the strike. He will want to be precise about its origins, its likely impact on other companies in the same industry and indeed on other related industries. He will be more interested than the previous two categories in the problem rather than the personalities involved in it.

Third, there is the time factor. Again, using the simple example above, the reporter from the local weekly probably will not be under much pressure; but the researcher/reporter from the television news programme and popular national daily will be in a considerable hurry. Cross-checking facts for accuracy will take second place to meeting the very tight deadlines both have. The industrial editor of the serious national daily will be under similar pressures, and possibly more so since his information needs are much less superficial.

Fourth, there is the type of story a journalist is working on. The crisis, like the example of the strike, usually places management in a defensive position where it has to react to rapidly changing events as well as to negotiate its way out of the crisis itself. No journalist will be inhibited in his need for information, or understanding of any failure to meet it, by something as irrelevant to him as the legal or insurance constraints on management's freedom to comment. These constraints will be very real in such cases as, for example, an explosion in a chemical plant where the cost of damage may be enormous and the insurance implications colossal. But there are many other types of news and feature stories not of a crisis nature where industrial management can and should satisfy the information needs and expectations of the press. Examples include an exciting technological breakthrough, a big export order, a new investment project.

In addition to satisfying these *ad hoc* demands, industry should attempt to develop a more continuous relationship with the media. It should do this to promote the best interests of the individual company and to assist a better understanding of the achievements and problems of industry as a whole. This does not mean turning a public relations department loose or churning out an endless stream of press releases. Neither does it mean spending vast sums of money on needless hospitality. Few journalists of any significance have the time or inclination for such things, and the events themselves do little to promote mutual respect and understanding between company and journalist. The essence of an effective on-going press relations programme rests on the following key factors:

1.   management understanding of the needs of the media and a genuine personal interest and flair among management at its most senior levels in dealing with the press;

2. an understanding of the limits of usefulness of a public relations
    department in a company's relations with the press. Aside from
    satisfying routine information needs, a public relations department
    should act as a catalyst, not a filter, for a company's communication
    with the press. A company's position on a given issue carries so much
    more weight if it is quoted in the media as coming from the managing
    director or factory manager rather than the ubiquitous 'company
    spokesman'. The very phrase smacks of propaganda and
    manufactured statement. In any event, the more experienced
    journalists frequently find their own ways of getting round the PR
    department if it fails to meet their needs;

3. a planned and clear appreciation of a company's objectives in its
    relations with the press. There is nothing sinister in this. It should
    ensure, among other things, that neither company nor journalist
    wastes time. Planning should identify the media, and specific
    journalists, with which a company wishes to have permanent
    relationship. The final selection will ultimately depend on personal
    chemistry. Either managing director X gets on with industrial
    correspondent Y or business editor Z or he does not. Forcing the issue
    will not help. If a senior manager is unable to strike up a healthy
    relationship with at least a few key journalists he should ask himself if
    it really is the rest of the world that is out of step!

One thing most journalists abhor is the obsequious public relations
man or general manager who tries false flattery, usually delivered with the
hand-wringing sincerity of the second-hand car salesman, in an attempt to
strike up a productive relationship. Comments like 'I think your paper is
absolutely the best. I read it every day', or 'Thank heavens we can talk to a
journalist who really understands our problems' as opening gambits are
usually the start of a conversation and a relationship that can go nowhere
but downhill.

A continued relationship with key journalists, who will in part be
selected, and in part be self-selected by the 'personal chemistry' of the
individuals involved, will depend largely on a company's ability to
provide:

1. easy access to information on:
    (a) individual company economic and social performance, future
        development plans and top management changes;
    (b) company innovations in management techniques and the social
        aspects of enterprise (labour relations, job enrichment projects,
        environmental impact, etc.);

(c) company achievements in research, exports, etc.;

2. assistance in developing industry trend data on such aspects as employment, pricing, export competitiveness, etc.;

3. opportunities for on- and off-the-record discussions with top management on broad issues of the day.

Journalists, especially those who specialize in such areas as business, industry and economics, have their own lists of preferred sources – companies, captains of industry and individual managers that can be relied on to provide full and honest information on a given subject. The type of relationship that can be developed over a period of time between a journalist and his preferred sources can be as immensely productive for the company as for the journalist – especially when a crisis erupts. It is not a question of expecting past favours to be returned. It is simply that, when a company faces a strike, takeover, possible nationalization or whatever, the attentions of a knowledgeable and responsible journalist can be exceedingly helpful.

Additionally, a company must not ignore the other sources of information available to a journalist, whether in a crisis or not. Apart from sources directly related to a particular event (perhaps a trades union, a competitor or a government department) there are two key sources that the media turn to as a matter of course: their own files on a particular company or industry, and the news agency wire services.

Most of the major media keep detailed files of press cuttings and other relevant information on the bigger or potentially newsworthy companies. (This, incidentally, is why any erroneous reporting on a company should be drawn to the attention of the newspaper or magazine concerned with a request that the correct information be placed on file – even if it is unnecessary or unwise to insist on a published correction.) News agency wire services are of increasing importance to the media as economic pressures restrict the use of staff journalists for every story that must be followed.

Individual crises can seldom be predicted (presumably, if they could, most would be avoided), but they can be anticipated to a certain extent. Wise management will have a set of contingency plans to meet the basic requirements of all parties likely to be involved, including the press. This is no different from any other form of insurance, like the provision of fire-fighting equipment in a chemical plant or safety equipment for workers doing a dangerous job. The cost in terms of having to repair the damage caused by misinformation or misunderstood fact can be exceedingly high. A company does not have to wait until the press is knocking at its front door to start developing some basic facts that will help to present a fair case for itself. 'No comment' will prove counter-productive unless there are genuine and explained legal or commercial reasons for taking this negative approach to the problem. A management that is prepared to be open and forthcoming in presenting its case will stand a far greater chance of achieving a fair presentation of its case in a crisis than the more usual situation, where the amount of information that management is prepared to divulge is in inverse proportion to the dimension of the crisis!

SECTION THREE

Practical guidelines for more effective communication

10. Issues and Options
11. Setting Realistic Objectives
12. Defining the Target Audience
13. Identifying the Message
14. Attitude Research
15. The Communications Armoury
16. Gearing Up for Better Communication

10

Issues and Options

So what are the practical options for business enterprise in Europe in the areas affecting its information and communication policy? In this section we shall take a look at some of the key issues, and some of the basic aspects of company communication policy and practice with which every senior manager should be familiar.

The central issues are clear.

1. Business enterprise is under attack throughout most of Europe, and even its right to exist in anything like its present form is being challenged in many countries. Much of this pressure is politically inspired and frequently based on unchallenged misinformation and innuendo. There is a collective responsibility for industrial management to take corrective action before the ideological battle, which is essentially one of communication, is finally lost.

2. The character of industry across Europe is changing rapidly to a participative form of industrial democracy – through social democracy in northern Europe and perhaps through some form of collectivism in the south. Harmonious participation depends upon a measure of basic understanding among the participants of the role of industry in the national social economic context. Again the catalyst is communication.

The non-commercial areas of business communication, that is to say communication activity not directly related to promoting the sale of a company's products or services, have consistently failed to attract adequate top management attention in any but crisis situations. Perhaps this has been largely because of their non-commercial nature. But the time is now long overdue for management at the very senior levels to focus on these issues because they are central to the survival, not just the future success, of business enterprise in Europe.

The character of industry in Europe has changed dramatically over the past two decades. The demands placed upon it by legislation, as also by political, economic and social pressures, have at once changed and multiplied. The result has been the emergence of a uniquely European brand of industrial democracy. It differs in character from country to country but it places a heavy reliance on the interdependence of social, economic and political policies. It also has a bias towards the participation of government and workers in the development and implementation of industrial policy. This involvement now far exceeds the scope and expectations of the stockholder.

There are powerful forces building up to coerce companies to disclose more information about their social and economic performance. These range from the broad guidelines for multinational corporations produced by the OECD to directives from the EEC Commission. Added to national legislation on statutory disclosure there are trades union and political pressures and the voices of a more investigative and better informed press. Whereas some forces are constructive and well intentioned, some are motivated by a dogmatic desire to 'expose' the prevailing economic system and ensure as a result that capitalism even in its attenuated European form is reformed out of recognition or abolished altogether. If business and industry has a credible story to tell, this added burden of communication should bring new life to the debate that can only be constructive. It is the historical reluctance of business to join the communication battle that has given heart to its adversaries and credence to their claim that business has more than a skeleton or two tucked away in the corporate cupboard.

There is a collective responsibility for industry as a whole to explain more effectively what can and cannot be done to solve social and economic problems. And a collective responsibility requires some resemblance of a collective response. Let us take the issue of profits as just one example. Industry has had its profits squeezed by taxation and other 'non-market' pressures to the extent that in some countries it had led to industry's under performance, to resulting unemployment, and to lack of export competitiveness. These almost entirely political pressures on profit are generally accepted, indeed called for, by public opinion because the level of profits and the uses to which they are put are both misunderstood and often deliberately misrepresented. A few well publicized examples of perhaps genuinely excessive profits and other manifestations of the 'unacceptable face of capitalism' and business is once more under attack as the root cause of many evils. The response of most companies to such attacks has been either to hope the problem will go away, or to justify inactivity on the grounds that there is nothing they can do about the problem on their own.

The problem has not gone away, and there is something industry can do about it, on both an individual as well as a collective basis.

Communication is fundamental to the successful functioning of a company in the participative context of industrial democracy. Communication from management must properly reflect the honest reality of company policy, and management as a whole must be receptive to communication from other participating or influential groups. Additionally, the changes in the character of industry in Europe which have created the need for this increase in the quality and quantity of communication have also created a need to adjust, broaden and change corporate policy itself.

These are manifestly not issues that management can delegate to specialists in public affairs or public relations. Communication policy and practice is an area that demands the same serious and systematic approach that management applies now to capital investment and product planning. Indeed, communication is in many ways more demanding and more critical than either of these – more demanding because identification of the right solution and assessment of success are much more difficult to quantify in the tangible forms management demands, and more critical because it is a central factor in the changing character of industry itself.

MANAGEMENT OPPORTUNITY

It is up to management to decide whether to regard Europe's emerging industrial democracy as a problem or to regard it as an opportunity. This will depend very largely on the imagination and adaptability of the individual. But one point is clear: the issues involved are too important for top management to delegate all or most of the area of communication to single specialists in this field.

The extent to which a company's reputation really affects its social and economic performance, and also its freedom of action, varies in different industries. For the company with objectives that are purely financial and short-term, reputation is probably of little significance. It is rare for the man-in-the-street to decide whether or not to buy from a particular company because of its general 'image'. The same is largely true of the purchasing agents of a company. These decisions are made on the basis of value for money, quality of product or service, delivery and competence. Boycotts organized by pressure groups to protest against the activities of companies, especially for political and sometimes social reasons, are seldom more than irritants to the company concerned.

However, it must be said that a company's reputation, especially on matters related to its political, social and (increasingly) environmental impact, does affect its stock market valuation and the morale of its work force. It affects a company's ability to recruit and retain good staff, especially for management positions. It affects productivity, absenteeism and a host of other factors essential to the successful operation of a business in anything but the short term.

There can surely be little doubt too that the reputation and image of industry in general can have, and has had, a dramatic effect on encouraging restrictive legislation, or in creating a climate of public sentiment in which such legislation is politically acceptable or even required. This is certainly a factor in legislation on corporate taxes, pricing and dividend restrictions, largely because it is widely assumed that these additional costs can be soaked up by the 'fat profits' that companies are assumed to make. It also applies to forms of enterprise such as banking, insurance and transportation, and is used to justify nationalization. Increasingly, Europe's socialist Left is calling for nationalization of industry's 'golden geese' and not merely the 'lame ducks' and industries of national strategic importance.

Of course, great care must be taken in assessing whether or not the bad reputation of a particular company, industry or business as a whole is justified in the present industrial context of Europe. If it is justified, then the solution is not to put more effort into communications or public relations but to begin planning some more fundamental change. This is a matter for an informed and objective management to decide.

PRIORITIES FOR ACTION

There are five fundamental aspects of company communication policy and practice that all managers must be concerned with.

One must be clear, first of all, about one's own company's overall objectives. This is not as easy as it sounds. Fundamental to industrial democracy is the need for all key participants (management, stockholders, workers and government) to agree broadly on what the overall purpose of industry is.

This does not mean, of course, that management's concept of company objectives should be smothered by those of the other parties involved. The European brand of industrial democracy depends very much on everyone understanding that there is a crucial difference between participation and control – the difference being much more than merely one of degree. However, it does very clearly rely a great deal on leadership. Indeed, in today's participative environment, true leadership by management is of more critical importance than ever before.

It is important, therefore, that a company's stated objectives should be an honest reflection of management's intent and not merely an attempt to tell stockholders, government and workers what management thinks each of these participants want to hear. Except occasionally in the short term, such a policy is bound to fail. Stated company objectives must bear scrutiny, critical appraisal and the passage of time. It is important too that a company's objectives should be communicated to all those who can influence their achievement. This action helps ensure the achievement of company policy and assists in the creation of a more favourable climate of opinion for business enterprise as a whole.

Communication priorities should be influenced by the scope of a company's objectives. Companies that have profit and growth as their sole objectives have a very different set of priorities from the company that has a broader set of corporate objectives (perhaps acknowledging that profit and growth are means to an end and not ends in themselves).

Second, management must decide which groups have a legitimate 'need to know' and which groups represent a potential problem. For most companies there is a growing legitimate 'need to know' (at least in the sense that it is being legislated for), especially by workers and government, in addition to the stockholder. Selection of priorities will of course be influenced by the kind of business a company is in – a manufacturer of television sets, refrigerators or automobiles will have consumer protection groups high on the priority list, while environmental protection groups will be high on the list of a manufacturer of chemicals and fertilizers.

It is clearly impossible to satisfy *all* the information and communication demands of all the groups we have reviewed in Section Two. To do so would not only place an unbearable burden of time, money and effort on a company, but would require a level of disclosure that might itself tend to eliminate freedom of enterprise. Further, unless the same levels of disclosure are generally accepted as standards on a world-wide basis, it would give those companies that continued to be selective a considerable if short-term commercial advantage.

The degree of information a company decides to communicate should be governed by fairly practical considerations like the effects on commercial competitiveness, contract discussions and labour relations; but these considerations should never be used (as they often are used) to justify a policy of minimum disclosure. The approach in terms of information to be disclosed should be one of 'how much can we give to satisfy the demands made of us?' and not 'how little can we get away with?' The latter policy destroys trust and credibility, both of which are essential qualities in effective management today.

The degree of information a company decides to communicate must also, as for any other business decision, be cost-benefit related. We must consider cost not only in terms of the financial outlay required for communication, but also, since information has a value to both giver and receiver, in terms of what benefits a company can expect to derive from communicating it. This is frequently the trickiest area for management judgement; but the soundest advice is never to look simply to the short-term impact. One other essential question we must ask in this context is whether or not the provision of a particular piece of information will improve understanding or merely add confusion. While this should never be used as an excuse for non-communication, it should at least condition the context in which the information is presented.

Ensuring that a company has the ability to meet the communication challenges of a potentially damaging crisis (a strike, factory explosion, take-over bid etc.) is of course vital, but, above all, communication policy and priorities should be seen in the context of an overall and on-going communications strategy and plan. While much of a company's communication has to be responsive to change, opportunity and crisis, it is quite wrong to conclude that most of a company's communication activity should be *ad hoc* and reactive. The result is inefficiency, confusion and misunderstanding.

One important safeguard here is the establishment of reporting systems to ensure that public attitudes towards the corporation are regularly and accurately monitored.

Finally, a company must recognize that effective communication is necessarily a two-way street. It involves listening, seeing and observing as well as transmitting information or an instruction. The failure of management to be a good observer of the environment, both internal and external, in which it must operate has perhaps indirectly contributed most to the poor overall reputation of industry. The relative deafness and blindness of management, be it due to arrogance or simply ineptness, has meant that much of its thinking is at odds with today's political and social realities. It has also created a situation in which much of what it wants to communicate is irrelevant or unintelligible to everyone but itself.

To use a financial analogy, the credibility current account of business went into the red some years ago. Considerable and concerted management effort will be needed to restore a credit balance. It may be years before business will be able to do what it should have done a decade ago: put some credibility on deposit for a rainy day.

11

Setting Realistic Objectives

Judging by the limited number of companies in Europe that can articulate their communication objectives beyond a vague and very general idea that they want to improve their image, there seems to be no general appreciation of the value of setting objectives in the communications area. Yet this surely must be the starting point for more effective communication. After all, if you do not know where you are going, any road will take you there!

A realistic set of objectives is as vital to successful communication as any other business activity, be it the production and sale of goods or the development of new products. Communication objectives provide management in general and the communication specialist in particular with a frame of reference and an agreed destination to work towards.

Perhaps the reason why most companies have not set themselves communication objectives is because to know how to reach somewhere you also have to know with some accuracy where you are at the moment – a company's current reputation with those that can influence its performance. Most companies just guess at this, and usually guess wrong.

A company's ability to establish this starting point on its own will vary enormously according to the size of the company and the group with which contact is to be made. For example, management of a company with 150 employees will probably have an accurate grasp of their workers' attitudes towards the company. Management of a large and possibly multinational company, on the other hand, will have to rely on information filtered up through layers of managers or to commission some formal attitude research. If the group is a large and influential one it is too risky to base everything on the opinions of individual senior managers whose perspectives may be affected by 'tunnel vision', personal prejudice and vested interest. Correct assessment of a company's current reputation, and an objective evaluation of the environment in which a communication programme may eventually be implemented, are first essentials without which the setting of objectives becomes a game of chance.

With the starting point established, however, with the greatest degree of accuracy that is practical, it then becomes possible to establish a realistic set of attainable communication objectives. The operative word here is 'attainable', because if they are not attainable they cannot be realistic. Of the many factors to be accounted for in the process of formulating them, the following six are important.

1. *The company's overall objectives and future development plans.* These may call for heavy external financing, the acquisition of other companies, the hiring of large numbers of people with particular skills, the closure of a factory or product line. Overall company objectives might include the provision of more jobs in a particular area, increased exports or an extension of worker participation. Whatever the mix, a company's objectives and future plans will influence the formulation of communication strategy, especially in terms of identifying the groups to approach and the type of information to impart.

2. *Management vision and style.* This point is closely linked to the previous one. The issue here is to what extent a company's senior managers themselves identify with expressed long-term company objectives, or whether they look only as far as their individual retirement dates or to the period they plan to stay in the company. The latter, often in the larger corporations, may well be prisoners of the short-term balance sheet and their personal careers, and care for little else. The shape of a company's communication objectives must take full account of the quality of all key corporate resources available to be deployed in their pursuit. The vision and style of top management is a vital conditioning factor.

3. *The company's business profile.* Is it labour- or capital-intensive; are its products consumer or capital goods, or does it provide a consumer or business service; how big are its markets in terms of geographical spread or numbers of customers? These factors will influence at least the selection of groups to approach, and their selection will in turn shape the overall objectives.

4. *Legal requirements.* A company is obliged to communicate certain types of information at a specific frequency to stockholders and various government departments throughout Europe, and to employees in a rapidly growing number of countries (six having been added in Europe during the last five years alone). With a continuous stream of directives from the EEC, guidelines from such groups as the OECD and local national pressures (coupled with a general reluctance by industry as a whole to go much further than legally required), more legislation in this area is inevitable. Wise management will anticipate its implications. Wiser management will treat legislated requirements as a minimum standard and not a norm.

5. *Reputation versus reality.* How accurate is the company's reputation with the various groups that can influence its future? A company may not be able to recruit enough of the right people because of a reputation for high employee turnover or poor working conditions. It may, because of some well published scandal in one country, be regarded with considerable suspicion by the government of another. It may be suffering from strikes and poor labour relations because it has a reputation among its workers for an indifference to their welfare and needs. If the reputation is inaccurate, communication will be vital to the solution, and may even be the solution.

6. *Company strengths and weaknesses.* Again, this point is closely tied to the previous one. If the key groups with which a company should communicate have been properly identified, and if their attitudes and interests have been properly assessed, management has the makings of a communication priority balance sheet. It should be in a position to determine a company's assets and liabilities in the eyes of those groups that are considered important to the achievement of overall company objectives – and to determine to what extent these strengths and weaknesses are known and understood.

A company's communication objectives should reflect the reality of the social, economic and political environment in which it operates, and represent a management commitment to a particular type and level of communication. Objectives should be cost–benefit-related, and ideally long-term. Above all they must be realistic in terms of the company's performance and overall objectives, and also in terms of the amount of time, money and effort that management can devote to their achievement. It is unwise to expect early or dramatic results. The communication programme may frequently have to overcome deep-seated prejudice as well as ignorance.

Objectives should indicate priorities, too, in terms of whom to communicate with and how much emphasis to give to each group.

Above all, perhaps, communication objectives, once agreed, should be committed to paper. There can then be no argument now or later as to what must be achieved. A written record is a constant reminder for all those involved in the task.

It is important that a company's communication objectives should not be established by public relations or other specialists in isolation and in ignorance of the broader issues affecting a company's overall objectives, economic and social performance. So, unless the communication specialist is already a member of the top management team (and a growing number of the more professional ones are these days), communication policy should be established by the chief executive directly with assistance from his communication, public relations and other advisers. This is the only way to ensure that communication objectives are in line with the spirit as well as the letter of company objectives. It also helps to ensure that top management as a whole understands and actively supports whatever communication programmes are developed to meet the objectives. A company communication programme without effective management support is a failure from the outset.

Communication objectives, however, are akin to overall company objectives in one other material respect. They need to be checked every now and then for relevance. A company that is happily pursuing the corporate objectives and policies it set for itself in, say, 1960 (assuming they were right then) is by definition heading in the wrong direction now. Similarly, a company's communication objectives and strategies must be adapted to the realities of the social, economic and political environment in which they are expected to take effect. This way, quite apart from their effectiveness in supporting overall company objectives, they will help shift the more general public debate on the future of business enterprise away from 'should capitalism be reformed out of recognition or abolished altogether?' towards a broader and more constructive question: 'how can the prevailing economic system be adapted to meet the needs of modern industrial democracy?'

12

Defining the Target Audience

In this chapter we shall look at a set of guidelines for identifying the 'target audience', who it is that company management must communicate with, on two bases: first in pursuit of individual company objectives, and second in the broader context of improving the climate for business as a whole.

Given unlimited resources, the list of groups and individuals with which a company could profitably communicate is dauntingly extensive. But a company's communication resources are finite, and management must be as ruthless in establishing priorities in terms of those with which it will communicate as in making, for example, an investment decision. Indeed, what we are talking about here is very much an investment in the future survival and success of an enterprise.

It is not a question of having to make a simple choice between a very open or restricted communication policy in a general sense. Management may well decide that the pursuit of its overall objectives calls for a very high 'profile' with, say, government and workers, but a very 'low' profile with the public at large. This will depend a great deal on the size of a company, whether or not its products naturally place it in the public eye, or whether it has had the spotlight thrown on it through accusation and scandal as with Hoffman–La Roche, ITT and Lockheed. Most companies, given the choice, do little about their reputation with the general public until forced to do so by events beyond their control. Unfortunately, the circumstances that place them in the public eye often reduce their stature or credibility to zero. They then have to build some foundations before they can even begin to think about getting their credibility account with the bank of public opinion back into the black again.

Given that top management at least has a clear appreciation of overall company objectives and their scope (which may be something of an assumption!), determining the individuals and groups with which a company should communicate is largely a question of determining who is in a position to help or hinder significantly the achievement of those objectives. The priority list should be determined with the same degree of formalized thought that goes into any other important management decision. No successful enterprise can survive for long if it applies as much hunch and guesswork to, say, marketing its products as most companies do to the non-commercial area of their communication activity.

What needs to be thoroughly analysed first is the potential impact of a number of groups on the achievement of company objectives – in the long as well as the short term. The list may include banks, institutional investors, private stockholders, customers, suppliers, local community leaders, business and trade organizations, senior executives in other companies, potential employees, Members of Parliament, government officials, trade union leaders, top management, middle management, other employees, consumer organizations, environmental organizations, teachers, students, international political and economic agencies, not to mention the general public. Obviously this list is not exhaustive, and many companies will want to extend or broaden it in certain areas to match their business profile and objectives. For example, a company manufacturing pharmaceuticals would need to add the Ministry of Health to the general category of government officials, as well as adding hospital administrators and doctors to the general category of customers.

For management that prefers to have things formalized, Table 9 (or some similar form) will be of some help. But whether this form is used or not, management will doubtless be surprised and dismayed by the end of this first phase of the exercise at the number of groups whose support is deemed to be important, very important or vital to the accomplishment of

Table 9

How important are each of these groups to:

1. Achievement of company objectives in the short-term?
2. Achievement of company objectives over next five to ten years?
3. The quality of the environment for business enterprise?

Write each of the numbers 1, 2 and 3 into the appropriate spaces for each group.

	Vital	Very important	Important	Helpful	Unimportant
Banks					
Institutional investors					
Private stockholders					
Customers					
Suppliers					
Community leaders					
Business/trade organizations					
Senior executives in other companies					
Potential employees					
Members of Parliament					
Government officials					
Trades union leaders					
Own top management					
Own middle management					
Other employees					
Consumer organizations					
Environmental organizations					
Teachers					
Students					
International political/ economic agencies					
General public					

company objectives. In fact, of course, a great number of individuals and groups are important to one degree or another to the success of a business enterprise. But clearly the next phase of the exercise must be to whittle the list down to a manageable group of absolute priorities that can command sufficient management attention.

The criteria that should be applied to the next stage should be based upon careful analysis of five factors.

1. What is the current attitude of each group to the company, and to what extent is this attitude based on inaccurate or insufficient information?

2. How much information related to the company does each group receive at the moment, and from whom? Management is by no means the only source of information for most groups, and information does not actually have to be accurate to gain acceptance.

3. What is the relative impact of information (from whatever source) on each group's ability and willingness to contribute towards the achievement of company objectives? In other words, how powerful is information and communication as a motivating factor for each group, and to what extent is a lack of accurate information a disincentive?

4. What are the information expectations of each group and how justifiable are they?

5. What level of information does each group actually need from management either to contribute fully to the achievement of company objectives or to prevent unnecessary hindrance to their achievement?

This process can perhaps be more easily completed with the use of formal analysis such as that suggested in Table 10. For the purpose of illustration, this table has been completed for the middle management of a hypothetical but not untypical medium-sized company. Indeed, we have deliberately picked middle management for this illustration because the information needs of this group, and the potential impact of information, are too frequently underestimated. In this case, attitudes towards the company are unhelpful, the group receiving little accurate information from anyone because it is squeezed between senior management (which regards the possession of information as a form of power over subordinates) and the shop floor (with which it has a poor relationship, each believing the other is underworked and overpaid). The conclusion is that the company could make this group much more productive in the pursuit of company objectives by satisfying their information needs and

Table 10

Group: company middle management	
Current attitude to company	Indifferent-to-negative. Minimal understanding of company policy or knowledge of/identity with company objectives.
Current information received/source	Low level of information on company achievements/problems from any source. Minimal communication with senior management or other workers. Biggest information source is rumour/grapevine.
Potential impact of information/ communication	Better understanding of company objectives/problems/achievements would be significant motivator.
Information expectations	Cynics expect no information. Most want more on company future plans, expected profits, explanation of company problems (factory closures, redundancies, etc), personnel policy and strategy.
Information needs	Better knowledge and understanding of company objectives/achievements/problems/future plans would improve identity with company, and encourage support for and pursuit of its objectives.
Action	Directors of personnel, industrial relations, and public relations to prepare detailed communication programme strategy and action plan within three months, after further consultation with middle management representatives.

thus creating a more positive sense of identity with those objectives. (It should also be noted, incidentally, that this group has a vital role in the process and success of worker participation.)

This kind of analysis, simple though it is, is almost certainly a task that no single manager can handle entirely on his or her own for all the groups that management has deemed important to the achievement of company objectives. Nevertheless, the job is probably best assigned to one individual to ensure some measure of comparability and objectivity. The individual selected must be sufficiently involved with top management to understand the true character and scope of company objectives. Alternatively, it must be an individual who is outside the company altogether who will not be subject to the prejudices and pressures that would apply to a staff man. The choice will depend on the quality of internal candidates for the task and the time they have available for it.

The exercise is well worth the effort, however, because it begins to take communication policy out of the realms of assumption, guesswork and hunch. Further, it provides management with data in a more tangible form. The process of formal analysis will indicate those groups to which management should pay particular attention – either because information, or the lack of it in an accurate form, has a significant impact on a group's willingness and ability to assist the achievement of company objectives, or because there is an existing 'communication gap' between the company and a group that already represents a problem.

At the very least the process of formal analysis should be applied to particular communication problem groups that have already been identified through some other means. Frequently the groups and the problems are related to an event, like a factory closure. In such a case workers will be a focus for communication activity – in addition to stockholders (who will want to know if their company is in a state of collapse) and the government (which will at least be concerned about the effect on unemployment statistics). Workers can, and should in such circumstances, be contacted directly. But in today's European environment of participative industrial democracy the discussions on why, when and how to close a factory will take place with worker representatives well before the final decision to proceed with the plan is taken.

In the first chapter of this section we concluded that, so far as short-term impact on a company's sales are concerned, the negative effect of reputation with external groups is usually negligible, but that industry's collective failure to respond to the communications war with those who advocate revolution has placed industry in a predicament that requires concerted and collective action, not merely collective moaning.

The task now confronting management in Europe, in addition to the need to adjust company policy to the requirements of a participative industrial democracy, is to ensure that the more influential groups on the priority list understand the economic facts and social realities of industrial life – and the practical alternatives.

Key target groups for this level of communication activity are workers and their representatives, government, the media, teachers and students. Clearly this is not a task for individual companies alone. For a start, it is only the bigger companies that will have the resources to implement an effective programme with all these groups. The smaller companies will need to focus their individual efforts on their workers and more local or specialized areas of government and education. The task is one that is particularly well suited to trade associations and industry federations. They should be in a position to present a broad picture of industry's achievements and be able to put its problems into perspective.

There has been far too little of this activity in most of Europe – partly because of a lack of competent staff and funding, and partly because of a lack of encouragement or support from member companies. Management must ensure that there is adequate authority and competence at association and federation levels to support individual company efforts to help create a new credibility and freedom for business enterprise.

13

Identifying the Message

Identification of what a company should communicate about itself is conditioned by four factors: the company's communication objectives, the horizon of interest of each group with which it wishes to communicate, an honest appreciation of company strengths and weaknesses within the scope of those interests, and the company's credibility with each group.

As we noted in Chapter 11, company communication objectives must be realistic to be attainable, and one of the realities to be recognized is that not everyone shares the same interests in a company as its management. Management will take pride in certain aspects of company achievements that will be totally irrelevant to others.

Let us look at two distinctively different groups to illustrate the point: employees at shopfloor level, and stockholders, both key participants in Europe's industrial democracy.

Employees at shopfloor level, aside from their official or elected representatives who need to take a broader view, have a horizon of interest in a company that rarely stretches much beyond the factory and community in which they work. As a consequence their information needs and expectations are quite narrowly personal. As many trades unions have discovered, it is extremely difficult to persuade workers to concern themselves with the interests of those in another location unless the outcome will affect their own personal lot. Their interests centre upon such issues as job security, job enrichment, pay and working conditions. They can be motivated to take an interest in the export achievements, expansion plans, profit levels and problems of the company as a whole only if these factors can be related to their personal lives and futures.

Precisely the same applies to other groups, including a company's stockholders. The only fundamental difference between the two is that stockholders invest their money and workers invest their time and labour – and within this context stockholders are able to move their contributed resource into and out of a company much more readily than a shopfloor worker. The stockholder is therefore less of a captive audience. Most private and institutional investors want to know that their money is safe and that it will grow. The state as an investor may well have broader politically motivated objectives but it will still seek a return of some kind on its investment. The investor's interests in a company's export achievements, expansion plans, profit levels and problems will thus be substantially different from those of shopfloor workers – and to be relevant, therefore, such information must be presented to each in a different (but definitely not contradictory) context.

Company strengths and weaknesses also play a crucial role in determining the kind of information a company should communicate. Self-evidently, management should throw the spotlight on a company's economic and social achievements, especially if these are relevant to the interests of its priority target audience. But a vital factor here must be the fourth key point we mentioned at the beginning of this chapter: credibility. Tempting through it may be, management must avoid being over-selective in the facts it communicates. The one essential ingredient that effective communication cannot dispense with is credibility, and the trust that this infers is the product of good past performance.

To achieve the required level of credibility, management cannot evade the necessity of a long-term policy of complete and open communication so that it can be trusted to give a complete account in both good times and bad. The credibility of business and industry, with very few exceptions, is currently at an all-time low, because companies have been traditionally reticent and highly selective, moreover, in the information that they have chosen to divulge. Perhaps the best, or at least that most consistent, example of company communication that lacks the level of credibility needed to do an effective job is the employee newspaper or magazine. Very few of these are much more than published management bulletin-boards with a little entertainment thrown in for balance. They report on company sales achievements, factory visits by the managing director, pep-talks from the board, births, marriages and retirements, and the odd feature on an employee growing a prize marrow. This is an unbalanced, high calorie–low protein diet – and is usually regarded with predictable disdain by those whose information needs it is presumably designed to serve.

There are three general categories of information that most companies need to communicate: explanatory, corrective and educative. All three types should form part of a consistent, planned, long-term communication programme. They will also be a part of a company's response to a sudden problem or opportunity.

Explanatory information puts company news and events into a relevant perspective for each group. An example of this, for instance, would be publication of a company's annual results. A company's profit or loss, sales, investments, etc., will need to be carefully explained if a company is to avoid being blamed for favouring one group's interests over another – stockholders complaining of too small a dividend, workers using an increased dividend to justify a higher wage claim, and local pressure groups using profit figures to ensure that more of the company's money is spent on anti-pollution equipment.

Most companies use corrective information because of a failure at the explanatory information stage – a 'reaction' necessitated by a failure to take effective 'preaction'. Corrective information, as part of a company's planned communication programme, should cover such aspects of the public debate on business enterprise that its adversaries have layered with popular misinformation and innuendo. As British Prime Minister James Callaghan once said, 'A lie can be half way round the world before the truth has got its boots on.'

The primary audience for corrective information in this context should be not only a company's employees, but also government officials, teachers and students. A good example here is the attack against multinational corporations that stand accused (and guilty by default) of milking foreign national economies, moving production around the world in search of cheap labour, using transfer pricing techniques to avoid taxation, causing currency fluctuations and even helping to overthrow unfriendly governments. It is however in this area of corrective information, which is tactically defensive in character, that the credibility of the communicator is of crucial importance. Industry must not necessarily speak with one voice on such issues, but some attempt must be made to ensure everyone is rowing in roughly the same direction – and pulling their weight! A measure of counter-attack should also be implicit in the use of corrective information, especially when it is used to counter an unreasoned attack.

The multinational corporation has been an easy target on three counts – it is usually big, seemingly impersonal, and by definition 'foreign' in the minds of most people. It has also been more lax than most in the public defence of its reputation beyond the national border of its home base. The well publicized criticisms of such companies as Lockheed, ITT and Hoffman–La Roche are assumed by critics to be the tip of the iceberg, with virtually no evidence to support such a sweeping generalization. Unchallenged rumour has become myth, and myth has become assumed fact. The multinational now faces questions of the 'when did you stop beating your wife?' type, with all their implied accusation and assumed guilt. The two case-studies on corporate advocacy in Section Four deal with this issue.

Educative information should be seen as part of a long-term communication programme. It is tactically more constructive and positive in character and is aimed at expanding the knowledge and horizons of interest of selected groups, and avoiding the need for after-the-fact corrective communication. Its task is to help build a better understanding and better climate for business enterprise on an individual as well as a collective basis.

This aspect of a company's communication policy relies very much on reasoned dialogue – not the rhetoric and emotion that is so much a part of the front-line battle between accusation, corrective information and counter-attack. Educative information should be directed primarily at the same groups as corrective information, but perhaps with greater emphasis on students who will make up tomorrow's employees, their teachers and government.

The communication programmes that most companies have developed and are working with now have a strong bias towards explanatory information because it is this type that is more directly related to the pursuit of an individual company's overall objectives. This activity must clearly grow in parallel with the needs created by the growth of a participative industrial democracy. The balance must shift, however, with increased initial emphasis on corrective communication and a build-up of constructive educative communication.

In a continent as inherently complex as Europe, multinational management must also realize that the information needs and horizons of interest of a single group will vary enormously from country to country. Taking workers again as the example (although the same applies to the media and other groups), their sophistication and interests in Germany and Scandinavia are very different indeed from those of Italy, Spain and Portugal. It is perhaps more than mere coincidence that in those countries where the key participants in the industrial system are more sophisticated and better informed there is less industrial strife and a much higher level of co-operation in the process of producing saleable merchandise.

Simple formal analysis, similar to that used for identifying the target audience in the previous chapter, is a sensible method of initiating the process of identifying what an individual company should communicate. For each primary target group, management must first identify what each considers to be its information needs, and its horizons of interest. Management must then determine to what extent it can meet those needs. Finally, what does the company want to say about itself, its problems and achievements, and how can it communicate this information in a context that will be relevant and credible to each group?

Table 11 illustrates one way of collating and presenting this information. For the purpose of illustration we have taken the same group as we did for Table 10 in the previous chapter (middle management of a medium-sized company). Use of Table 11 takes the process of formal analysis one stage further, and only one stage removed from the final step, which is to decide which communication vehicle to use to ensure the information is received and understood.

In the broader context of defending business enterprise and helping to

Table 11

Group: company middle management	
Horizon of interest	Primarily interested in the unit (e.g. factory) in which they work; but want to see this in the context of company policy/problems/achievements as a whole.
Information needs	Better knowledge and understanding of company objectives/achievements/problems/future plans would improve identity with company and encourage support for and pursuit of its objectives.
Key message points	– Company social/economic contribution to local community. – Explanation of overall company economic/social objectives and achievements to date. – Current company problems and their social/economic implications. – Company future plans, especially in relation to local unit. – Economic facts of enterprise (role of profits, etc.).

build a healthier climate of opinion for business and industry, companies (both individually and collectively, through trade associations and industry federations) must be much more assertive in explaining their achievements and problems. The importance and purpose of profits are seldom explained in terms that are relevant and intelligible to the vast majority of workers, or to students in the process of choosing a career. Business has permitted its antagonists free reign in attacking the prevailing economic system. Industry stands idly by while unemployment is blamed on the failure of capitalism, as if other factors (including government policy) were not at least equally involved.

This is not to say, of course, that company profits are always reasonable and explainable, or that industry is faultless, or that the prevailing economic system is not in some measure to blame for such social problems as unemployment. But the correct solutions to these problems will always elude us if the debate on the issues involved is so hopelessly one-sided. Industrial management must play a much greater role in the now crucial debate on its future.

14

Attitude Research

In previous chapters of this section we have urged management at the senior levels to get much more directly involved in the development of company communication policy, and to practise a kind of 'communication-by-objectives'. We have pointed out, a blinding glimpse of the obvious, perhaps, that an essential prerequisite to the formulation of realistic and attainable objectives is to know where one is starting from. Further, a company needs to be sure during the process of reaching the stated objectives that it continues to head in the right direction. A company also needs to evaluate the relevance of what it communicates in the context of the information needs and horizons of interest of each 'target group'.

Guesswork and hunch are the least reliable of tools for these assignments. Attitude research is about the only satisfactory answer. The cost in both time and especially money can be high, but the cost of not using it in terms of wasted time and money is usually very much higher. Many companies in Europe (and this is much less so in the United States) justify a failure to use attitude research on the basis that their communication budget is small and they cannot afford it. In reality it is these companies that need research most because they cannot afford to waste a single penny, centime or pfennig of their limited budgets. All too often, however, it is communication specialists and public relations people themselves who avoid the use of research, especially to measure the effectiveness of communication programmes, because they are not confident that the results will justify their existence. Management should insist on at least some occasional measurement of company achievements in the communication area.

It is important, however, to realize the limitations of attitude research and accept that it is no substitute for management imagination and professional innovation. It will not provide answers; it will merely establish the framework within which answers may be found.

Of the three types of research assignment that we have identified, the first two – identifying the 'starting position' and checking progress towards the objective – generally require a similar approach. The purpose is management control, and the emphasis is on obtaining reliable information about the target group's awareness of, and attitudes towards, the company and its competitors.

To achieve reliable research results, it is often necessary to obtain systematic information from large numbers of the target group. So that the information collected on such a scale can be handled statistically, use is generally made of structured questionnaires and carefully designed procedures for administering them. This is a specialized business, and is normally carried out by either the company's research department or, more often, an outside agency.

Research is often used to measure the effectiveness of particular communication campaigns. For this purpose it is essential to carry out surveys before as well as after the activity, and if possible at least twice before, so that the campaign can be evaluated against existing trends. We stress this point because, although it may be obvious to everyone concerned, it is surprising how often it only becomes obvious half way through the campaign! Moreover, the surveys must be fully comparable in design and execution, otherwise the findings will be difficult to compare.

But however well conducted the research, short-term shifts in awareness and attitudes are difficult to evaluate. Seasonal factors, product promotions by the company and its competitors, major news items and economic and social changes can all affect attitudes, and it is often difficult to isolate the effect of promotional activity from that of other, uncontrollable market forces. However, two things can be done to help management in this task. First, the 'before' and 'after' surveys should be carried out, if possible, under similar levels of overall company activity. Because the trade and promotional activity of most companies follows an annual cycle, this often means in practice repeating the research at exactly the same time of year. Second, it will be helpful to keep a comprehensive diary of all events that might affect awareness or attitudes, before, during and after the campaign, so that all relevant factors can be included in the evaluation of the research findings.

The same points apply where a company has a continuous communication programme, and conducts regular research to monitor its effectiveness. What it amounts to is that research is always least useful when it is carried out as an afterthought to a campaign, and most useful when it is planned into the communication programme from the start and is regarded as an integral part of it.

How the research is commissioned is of critical importance. The quality of the research will depend very largely on the quality of the brief given to the research agency. Indeed the brief, which should set a precise framework and objectives for the research, will not just determine the quality of the research, but will also have a major influence on the structure and the methods used (postal questionnaire, telephone or personal interviews, or any of the available alternatives).

For the opinion research conducted for chapter three, a written brief (Table 12) was prepared and discussed in detail with both Nick Winkfield of Landell Mills Associates, who designed and conducted the research, and Management Centre Europe, who co-operated in the project. It was decided to split the sample of chief executives to be questioned into two matched sub-samples – one to be asked questions about current practice and the other to be asked about the optimum policy for industry as a whole. The reason for this, quite simply, is that one cannot expect the individual being questioned to wear two hats and objectively express views on what industry should be doing while at the same time outlining what his company does at the moment. His answers to one will strongly influence his answers to the other. This decision immediately doubled the size of the sample, and thus exercised a strong influence on the choice of research method.

It was, of course, an unusual piece of research. But there is a valid lesson to be learned: before deciding on the research method it is necessary to analyse the objectives carefully, keeping in mind the likely reactions of the target group when faced with different types of questions.

The research methods considered were face-to-face interviews, telephone interviews, and postal questionnaires.

Research based on face-to-face interviews, conducted by skilled and appropriately qualified interviewers, is by far the best way to tackle more complex issues where qualitative factors are important to the value of the research. It is only in a personal interview, where the interviewer has the opportunity to dig beneath the surface of simple answers to simple questions, that research of any real depth becomes possible. The problem is that a large number of people need to be interviewed to avoid the risk of bias in the results. Most research based on the views of less than 80 to 120 (depending on the subject of the research) will be statistically suspect, however pertinent the findings may be. (When it comes to researching the views of a whole nation, at the time of a general election, for example, the minimum numbers may swell to 1,000 in a country like Holland and as much as 2,000 in a country the size of Britain, Germany and France.)

The cost of arranging and carrying out an adequate number of face-to-face interviews with chief executives would have exceeded available funds by an embarrassing margin, however, and this method was therefore ruled out for our research.

Table 12

The Research Brief

Background

We are engaged in writing a book about industrial policies and strategies for the dissemination of information. One section of the book will rely heavily on a research survey carried out among chief executives in the four major industrial nations of Europe.

Objectives

1. To ascertain a consensus view of chief executives in Europe's four biggest industrial nations (Britain, Germany, France and Italy) on an optimum corporate policy for the dissemination of information to various key 'publics' (and to measure the 'distance' between this optimum corporate policy and current corporate practice).

2. To ascertain the chief executives' perception of the importance of communications (actual and trend) as a management tool.

3. To determine the priority 'publics' and the chief executives' perception of them.

4. To determine the kind of information the chief executive feels each 'public' should be privy to.

Notes

1. A comprehensive list of chief executives will be available from which the sample may be drawn.

2. The sample should be large enough to allow confident statistical interpretation, probably on a country-by-country basis as well as in total.

3. The survey design should as far as possible allow respondents to express themselves freely on the subject matter of the research, and not restrict them to a choice of pre-determined answers.

Timing

The report on the survey must be submitted by February 1977 at the latest, to enable us to meet the publisher's deadline.

Cost

A budget has not been set for this project, but economic considerations are of prime importance.

Telephone interviews had several advantages: they cost less than face-to-face interviews, they allow probing on key questions, they can be carried out quickly, and this particular target group – chief executives – all have telephones. But the telephone interview has to be kept short (European businessmen, unlike their American counterparts, are peculiarly reluctant to express themselves at length to strangers on the telephone), and certain of the questions to be included would have caused serious problems.

Postal questionnaires are slow, the response rate is generally much lower than with personal contact, and they do not allow probing ('What do you mean by . . . ?', 'anything else?', and so on). But they do allow one to ask quite complex questions, and – particularly important with members of this target group, who may be genuinely interested to give their views, but are dealing with a crisis at the precise moment when the researcher calls upon them – they can be completed whenever the recipient wishes. Moreover, they are relatively inexpensive to administer.

In view of all these factors, it was decided to use a four-page postal questionnaire, which was mailed to the chief executives under the cover of a full explanatory letter. Of course, different problems require different solutions, and the theoretically ideal solution is most often economically impossible. What matters in planning communication research is to build it into the overall communication programme from the start, to be absolutely clear about research objectives, and to make sure that the researcher (internal or external) is equally as clear about them.

But a more flexible approach is often needed to explore the information needs and motives of the target group in depth. This knowledge is needed by the writers and designers of press releases and advertising material, for whom it provides valuable raw material for their creative work.

A variety of sophisticated techniques can be used to reveal people's emotional reactions to creative material, to determine for example how much of an advertisement they read before getting bored with it. Pre-testing of individual communication projects, by means either of esoteric electronic gadgetry or of simple interview or group discussion techniques, is in fact a relatively inexpensive type of research – and worth its weight in gold when a company is about to launch a high-cost project like corporate advertising or a new corporate magazine.

Research is in some ways like a map and compass in the desert. Without it one can waste a lot of time and effort going round in circles, or can even get dangerously lost. With it, provided its limitations are understood, one knows where one is starting from, where to head for and how far one can expect to reach with a given communication vehicle in a given time.

15

The Communications Armoury

Having set communication objectives, and identified what a company wants to communicate to which groups, management must be familiar with the vehicles at its disposal for delivering the communication. This aspect of implementing communication policy is more properly left to the communication specialist, but every general manager should be aware of the relative strengths and weaknesses of the tools being used for the job in the same way that every good general should be aware of the characteristics of the weapons in use. Otherwise he cannot exercise the same measure of control over the course of the battle.

Communication techniques and devices can be compared to weaponry in many ways, in fact. There is the eyeball-to-eyeball communication between manager and critic, for example, when both are able to use the verbal bayonet to greatest effect. There is the larger meeting situation where one or two managers face an audience of fifty to a hundred where the rifle and hand-grenade of carefully directed exhortation or merely explanation are most suitable because the target is readily identifiable and visible. At the other extreme, where the target is large, dispersed, and not too easy to identify, the high-intensity nuclear warheads of television and press advertising may be the right weapon to project the company viewpoint – even though the cost in money terms is high and a lot of the ammunition may be wasted. With all but the simplest of communication problems, however, a careful 'mix' of weapons will be needed for a communication campaign.

Face-to-face communication, be it on a person-to-person basis or with one person addressing an audience of 1,000 or more, is widely felt to be the most effective method of conveying information. Historical precedents for this assertion range from Cicero to Hitler; and, to be sure, such men are dramatic examples of the art. But this particular weapon, like the high-velocity rifle, is only as effective as the person operating it. With the right finger squeezing the trigger it can be devastating; in the wrong or in inexperienced hands it is at best a waste, and probably counter-productive. Before any manager uses this particular weapon himself, or encourages another to do so, he must be made aware of his individual skill with it – and, if in any doubt, must get some training in how to use it. Poor face-to-face communication leaves the message unreceived and the communicator stripped of future effective authority. He may even become, as a result, a preferred target himself. Many company chairmen and managing directors have won or lost these positions partly on the strength of their ability to use the face-to-face communication technique.

Press relations is another area where the personal skills of the communicator (be it managing director or public relations specialist) are almost as important as the interest and honesty of whatever it is his company wants to communicate – and not only because it frequently involves face-to-face communication. There are two aspects to be considered here: first, the effectiveness of communication from company to journalist, and second, the effectiveness of individual media to project the communication to the desired target audience. It is not quite as hazardous as having to ricochet a bullet off a wall to hit the target in question; but at best there is a filter applied to what the company is attempting to communicate. The filter consists of the individual journalist's perception and prejudice (however subconcious) and the credibility of the medium he represents. President Jimmy Carter found this out when he gave his famous interview on his views on morality and related issues in *Playboy* magazine during the 1976 presidential campaign: in *Newsweek* or the *New York Times* a similar interview would have had an entirely different, and probably positive, impact.

In addition to using the press as a communication vehicle for whatever a company wants to communicate in support of its overall business objectives, management must also pay more attention to the role of the media, both printed and broadcast, in the broader context of creating a more favourable climate of opinion in which business and industry must operate. Even in those countries where the media is most sophisticated (like Germany, Britain and France), business leaders criticize it for its attitude towards business. If business leaders really feel they are misrepresented, a major element of the solution is in their hands. It is no good merely bleating that few journalists have any practical experience in industry and therefore cannot hope to understand it properly – this is a reality that management must face, and against which it must provide. The media do not always criticize business and its leaders out of a perverse sense of fun or mischief.

Perhaps the best example of the communication explosion since World War II, expecially in terms of technological advance and speed, is television – an absolute minefield for anyone wanting to project anything more subtle than a simple non-controversial message. Only the most skilled and well trained individuals should allow themselves to be featured on 'the box' in anything remotely approaching a dilemma, let alone a crisis. This is not an excuse for not doing it, however; it is a reason for mastering this most difficult and powerful of media. In weaponry, television (apart from television advertising) is a highly sophisticated nuclear device, with a hair-trigger, and no time-fuse at all that permits the user to take corrective action at the time of detonation. ('I am sorry, what I really meant was . . .' is fine to correct a misunderstanding with a newspaper reporter; but it does not look good on television!) It is only safe in the most skilful of hands.

There is one fairly safe, and highly effective, use of television, however – and that is the use of closed-circuit or video recorded television for internal communication. Many companies have used this to enormous effect, and its relatively high cost must of course be measured in the context of its effect. Here, again, its use requires an understanding of the medium and a basic empathy with the concept of personal communication. Properly used, however, it can carry with it the impact and credibility of a personal appearance (because of the role television plays in most people's lives), while reaching a theoretically limitless audience fairly immediately, anywhere in the world.

In the same general area, films and other audio-visual devices can play a useful role especially in communicating what we have referred to in a previous chapter as educative information. Curiously, but again primarily because of the role television plays in most people's lives, a film does not have the intensity of communication impact that seeing the same thing on 'the small screen' does. A film is somehow artificial, at least once removed from real life and the reality that the viewer has to live with on a day-to-day basis. Additionally, of course, most people feel that films are much more controllable for the purposes of propaganda. Their role, therefore, is not naturally at the battle-front, but more as strategic back-up.

Because of the unreliability or ineffectiveness of newspapers, magazines and the broadcast media to say exactly what companies wish to have said about themselves, or (perhaps less cynically) because no public medium exists primarily to encourage the pursuit of an individual company's overall objectives, many companies create their own media. Which company of any size does not produce an employee newspaper or magazine? Virtually no company, whatever the size, lacks a bulletin board (and a bulletin board is as much a medium of communication as an employee newspaper). Many companies sponsor external magazines too, and few companies miss the opportunity of the statutory annual stockholders' report to promote some corporate virtue or other. 'Sponsored print' is, for all the cynicism frequently heaped upon it, an entirely valid and often most effective weapon of communication. It lacks the credibility of third-party endorsement in some ways, but it represents a public and permanent record of commitment to a particular policy or point of view. The pity of it is, however, that nothing like enough effort and thought usually goes into planning their content to ensure they are read. They tend to reflect management's interests and not the needs and interests of those to whom they are directed. Considerable sums of money are thus wasted with little benefit beyond giving management a nice warm feeling.

One of the potentially more useful examples of 'sponsored print' is the corporate report – an extension of the annual report to stockholders, which includes a social as well as economic audit of a company's performance. It is a tool that an increasing number of companies are considering using to help meet some of the information needs of other groups including workers and their representatives, government, special interest groups of relevance to the company's activities and others. In theory, the corporate report accepts two communication needs that the annual report to stockholders has traditionally never sought to meet:

1. the need for a company to report publicly and formally to other groups to which it has a (moral if not legal) responsibility, in addition to the stockholder;

2. the need for a company to report publicly and formally on qualitative (social) as well as quantitative (economic) aspects of its activities and impact.

The principles of both points are relatively easy to accept for all but the most conservative of managements. They are much more difficult to put into practice, however, especially the latter. There are established formulae for reporting on a company's economic performance, based on the disclosure of quantifiable fact. There are no established guidelines for reporting on a company's social impact. The factors involved are related to intangible values such as the quality of life, working conditions, environmental impact and so forth. Some companies have made considerable efforts to produce a comprehensive corporate report. None have yet found a universally acceptable formula, and it is clear that a great deal of innovation and experiment has yet to be undertaken in this area. Industry would be wise, however, to take the lead in finding a solution itself, rather than wait for public opinion and legislation to overtake it once more and insist on reporting criteria that it may find difficult to comply with.

It has often been said that 50 per cent of the money spent on advertising is wasted – but no one has found a way to determine which 50 per cent. In the case of corporate advertising the wastage rate is probably as high as 80 per cent – and a lot of it is fairly obvious. Remarkably little corporate advertising starts life with a specific communication objective. In fact, it very often begins with the chairman or managing director wanting some advertising around annual meeting time almost on a 'keeping up with the Jones's' basis. What is produced usually winds up being an ego trip for the man at the top. If a corporate advertising campaign is lucky enough to start life with a more laudable and more precise purpose, the effect is usually dissipated by a company wanting to buy big spaces, even whole pages, to attract attention and then insisting on having its money's worth by filling the space with words and possibly a few irrelevant pictures. This happens, of course, because management wants to squeeze the maximum possible out of the original high investment, and because of an entirely false assumption that others share the same degree of interest as management in the company's activities and achievements. Corporate/institutional advertising is, however, the controlled nuclear device of communication in terms of the scale of its potential effectiveness. Properly directed and contained, it can have a most dramatic effect – especially if it is used to communicate solid demonstrable fact. The weapon is not subtle or inherently credible enough to convey nuances of meaning or opinion.

No review of communication weaponry would be complete without specific reference to the written word, as opposed to the media that carry it. After all, the word is the war-head and the media simply the means of its delivery. It is the use of words, or rather their misuse, that causes even the best planned communication programme to fail. The simplest message can be thoroughly obscured by the words selected to express it. The simple becomes complex, and the complex unintelligible.

A few decades ago an American calling himself a 'readability counsellor' invented a system for evaluating the readability of written text.

It is a points system based on the average number of words in sentences and the number of words with three or more syllables. He called it the Fog Index. The same system was taken up by the Staff Training Centre in Britain, where it was renamed the Clarity Index. Most newspapers have a Clarity Index rating of about thirty – sentences with an average length of twenty words and 10 per cent of the words with three or more syllables.

The system proves the law that governs most industrial communication: *The more important the message, the more complex its delivery.*

Take a brace of inter-office memoranda and prove the point for yourself. The *Sunday Times* did earlier this year at the end of one of British Leyland's worst industrial disputes. It analysed several of the company's management memoranda to employees. One crucial memo to workers, an ultimatum concerning productivity, had a Clarity Index rating of over fifty. The only management memo analysed that fell below thirty was one wishing all employees a happy new year. Sadly, British Leyland is the rule rather than the exception in this area of industrial communication.

In many parts of this chapter we have used military metaphors and likened communication techniques and devices to weapons. The analogy is entirely valid for industry's response to its critics. But in the context of worker participation and industrial democracy, where the ultimate ambition is balance and harmony, such implied aggression will often prove counter-productive – however defensive its origins. Many of the same communication methods and devices must be used, of course, but their tone and the manner in which they are used must clearly avoid the continuance or, worse, creation of an adversary mood.

In both contexts, however, there are three crucial 'devices' that all managers must use to achieve effective communication: their ears, eyes and personal sensitivity. Any manager, but especially a senior or chief executive, must apply his wits and intelligence to observation as well as the expression of a particular thought, opinion or instruction. He must be an expert observer for two reasons. In the first place it will help him position the thought, opinion or instruction he wants to communicate in a context that will make it understandable and acceptable to the individual or group to whose attention it is directed. In the second place it will help him avoid considerable and unnecessary frustration by keeping his thinking and behaviour adjusted to the environment in which he must operate – be it the handful of people who report directly to him, the department, factory or company for which he is responsible, or the relationship of his business conduct to the world at large.

Recognition that communication is a two-way street is an essential prerequisite to effective communication in virtually any circumstance. Many managers develop a desire to express themselves more effectively, but many fewer employ the necessary skills and sensitivities to listen and observe objectively.

In this chapter we have reviewed briefly some of the key characteristics of the potentially more effective methods of communication. A planned communication programme will use a mix of most of these, the weight being given to each depending upon the objectives of the programme, the size and diversity of the target audience, the message to be communicated and the funds available. These factors will be conditioned by the determination with which a company gears up for more effective communication, an issue with which we deal in the next and final chapter of this section.

16

Gearing Up for
Better Communication

For most companies the decision to gear up for much more than a routine level of communication activity (that required by law or current local custom) is a major one. Except in those cases where a company is planning only for increased communication with a closely defined group like the government, its consequences are so publicly visible that, once taken, the decision is difficult to reverse without considerable loss of face. Even with less public groups than government a reversal of the decision is at least an embarrassment, and potentially much worse.

It must be a deliberate decision, therefore, with a clear understanding of its positive purpose and implications as well as the potential dangers. The decision should be based on a company's ability to bring these factors to bear:

1. a clear sense of relevant direction for the new policy;
2. a will to communicate, shared by at least most of the top management team;
3. provision of adequate resources to support the new policy – people, money, and management involvement.

As we have indicated elsewhere, a company's communication activity must be relevant to the needs and horizon of interest of those to whom it is directed for it to have any positive effect at all. It must also reflect, or at least not be at odds with, the overall philosophy and objectives of the company. This means that there must be some harmony between a company's objectives and the needs and interests of the various groups with which it is to communicate. If this harmony does not exist, communication beyond the limited aim of actually achieving this harmony of basic objectives can be dangerously counter-productive. In most such cases, communication will not be the answer. Indeed, the words of one song that was very popular in 1976 and 1977, 'communication is the problem to the answer' may prove to be correct. The answer itself will more likely be some changes in company policy and objectives.

But let us assume that company policy is relevant to needs and expectations beyond those of the stockholder. Let us assume that management wants to keep a step ahead of legislation and the minimum requirements of local customs in the area of disclosure of information. Let us assume further that management has the will to accept the twin communication challenges of the trend towards industrial democracy and the increasing pressures on freedom of enterprise. What resources and other support must a company then provide to gear up for more effective communication?

These will of course vary considerably from company to company according to its size, the nature of its business and any actual problems it may currently have or be expecting. There are, however, a few common denominators that can be applied – especially in the area of people, organization and management involvement in the function.

The function sails under a number of flags – but usually can be described by a combination of words, one each from the following columns:

Corporate	Affairs	Director
Public	Relations	Manager
External	Communications	Officer

The choice of words in the last column usually indicates the status of the function within the organization. The choice of words in the middle column seldom indicates anything, but when it does it is usually a subtle reference to the breadth of the function ('Affairs' being broader than 'Relations', which is in turn broader than mere 'Communications'). The same applies to the first column, especially in American companies where the word 'Corporate' tends to cover both internal and external audiences while 'Public' frequently means just external.

In fact, the distinctions mean far more to the holders of the titles than to anyone else – practitioners of the function are no different from any other in this respect. However, we shall refer to the function henceforth as 'Corporate Affairs'.

The position of the corporate affairs function in the organization hierarchy is a key determinant of its likely effectiveness. Because it touches many other functions within the company it must be privy not just to overall company policy, but to management's strategic and tactical decisions in pursuit of policy as well. An effective corporate affairs function will spend half its time communicating with non-management groups about the company and the other half of its time helping management to understand and adapt/relate to the often changing needs and expectations of those groups that affect company performance.

For these reasons the function must be an integral part of the top management team. The chief executive must not compromise on this, or on his selection of a specialist to lead the effort. The function generally has not achieved the status in Europe that it has in the United States, but the trend over the past decade has been very much in this direction. One of the problems that the function has is that its growth, in sheer numbers of practitioners as well as in importance, has created a vacuum of professional competence. In the 1950s the function, where it existed, was usually in the hands of an ex-journalist or someone (salesman, engineer or administrator) who had become surplus to everyday company requirements. They were given the sinecure of 'public relations'. The go-go years of the 1960s saw the period of greatest growth for the function. Having a full-time PR staff became a very fashionable corporate status symbol. But what it achieved in quantity it over-compensated for with a lack of professional quality. In the 1970s, as the function has become a management necessity rather than a 'nice-to-have' management option, the corporate affairs function has necessarily grown in professional competence and effectiveness and has increasingly achieved top management status.

Necessity pulled the function out of the chicken-and-egg problem of not being part of the top management team because it was contributing little to company performance, and of not being able to contribute because of its exclusion from management's upper reaches.

> The function is moving away from blatant advocacy and justification of a company posture and viewpoint towards a more subtle role of helping company management understand the environment in which it operates and the likely impact of company actions [says Peter Earl, 1977 president of Britain's Institute of Public Relations]. Increasingly now it is becoming an integral part of the top management team, sometimes at board level.

The 1977 president of Germany's Public Relations Association, Martin Duerbaum, takes the point a stage further:

Because of its current status and role as a catalyst, especially in those countries that have a participative form of industrial democracy, the corporate affairs function now attracts some very talented men and women – not only from universities and business schools, but from other senior functions in a company as well. But there is a demand, above all, for an intensified professionalism – the days of the 'PR amateur' are over!

The selection of individuals to fill the corporate affairs function in the top management team, either by promotion or by external recruitment, is perhaps more crucial than for any other function except that of chief executive. A company naturally wishes to have the highest levels of professional competence in its top management team in all functions; but with corporate affairs some additional qualities are required. To do the job effectively the senior corporate affairs specialist either must be in fairly total sympathy with the policy, style and behaviour of the company, or must be in a position to help management change them. This is far less crucial for, say, the legal or finance functions. The corporate affairs specialist who offers his professional competence to any company in any circumstances, like a mercenary, will be of much less value to a company with any real personality or any genuine desire to achieve more than a superficial understanding with the environment in which it operates.

This is why a company's top corporate affairs specialist is often more vulnerable than most others when there is a change of chief executive.

The top corporate affairs specialist must also have a good working knowledge of, and contact with, the groups whose support is most essential to the achievement of company objectives. In making the appointment, the chief executive should also be satisfied that the scope and potential of the job are in keeping with the skills and expectations of the man or woman being considered. A corporate affairs specialist who is over-qualified can be as much of a problem for the chief executive as one who is under-qualified. The former is more likely than the latter to withdraw as a candidate, but neither should be encouraged.

All of this assumes, of course, that the chief executive has a clear idea of the kind of corporate affairs job he feels needs to be done; but what qualities should a chief executive look for in a corporate affairs specialist if he has little or no idea of these needs? The answer must be not to look for any. Do not look for a corporate affairs specialist at all. Until the chief executive has some appreciation of the job that must be done he cannot possibly know what qualities and skills to look for.

There is a positive role here for external corporate affairs counsel.

While most call themselves public relations consultants and are generally oriented towards support of marketing and other corporate advocacy programmes, there are a few whose expertise and experience extend to the breadth of the corporate affairs function. These individuals can be a significant aid to the chief executive in assessing a company's communication needs.

In addition to their more traditional role of fulfilling the external communication needs of companies that either do not need or cannot afford a full-time staff for the function, or as a back-up for the staff of larger companies, corporate affairs and public relations counsel are increasingly used for what they call 'ad hoc issue-oriented programmes'. This means providing specialist help in solving problems with environmental and consumer pressure groups or even with government. This trend is particularly marked in the United States, and is becoming increasingly true for Europe as well.

The level of financial resources required to support an effective communication programme will vary considerably from company to company. Here there are no rules or guidelines related to percentage of sales or any factor other than the job to be done. The normal commercial rules of 'getting what you pay for' apply to some extent, but it is an opportunity for considerable wastage. Remarkably few companies exercise a degree of management control sufficient to reduce its unnecessary excesses. Some of the larger multinational companies spend tens of millions of dollars every year on non-marketing communication programmes, but too few use adequate control techniques to ensure maximum cost–benefit effectiveness. It has to be acknowledged, of course, that the effectiveness of the type of communication we are talking about here is never as easy to measure as the output of a machine or a factory. Attitudes and opinions, and above all their effect, are infuriatingly intangible commodities. But management at least must ensure that the projected cost of a proposed communication programme is related to an attainable set of objectives, and that some attempt is made to measure the degree to which those objectives are achieved. Both of these points are covered in earlier chapters.

Direct involvement of the entire top management team in the development and implementation of communication activity is vital to its success, except in the case of very narrowly based programmes affecting one or two closely defined groups. It is essential for three reasons.

1. Management involvement is central to one of the key points we mentioned at the beginning of this chapter – the will to communicate. This is very much a question of the corporate state of mind and an

acknowledgement of the need to communicate. It is part of the chief executive's function to ensure that this spirit and commitment is fostered.

2. Virtually all functions will be key conduits in the 'receiving' phase of an effective two-way communication programme.

3. All functions will be affected directly or indirectly by company communication programmes. They should therefore be involved in the definition of the communication problem (or opportunity) as well as the development and implementation of solutions. Industrial relations, personnel and administration departments will need to be closely involved in any programme related to employees, for example, and both legal and marketing functions may need to be integrated into at least the planning of programmes related to government.

Gearing up for more effective communication activity requires above all management commitment – a commitment of adequate resources, but mostly a commitment of intent. The level of this commitment will depend on management's understanding of the need to communicate, and this will also determine the ultimate success or failure of any communication activity.

SECTION FOUR

Case-studies on the power of communication

17

Worker Participation

Philip Rosenthal is one of Europe's most enterprising entrepreneurs. As chairman and chief executive of Rosenthal AG he has transformed the company his father founded in 1879 from a small manufacturer of chinaware to an internationally known producer of high-quality glass, ceramics and furniture as well. He has also done more than perhaps anyone, as a politician as well as an industrialist, to change the character of German industry – in one respect at least: his commitment to the industrial logic of worker participation in the management and ownership of business enterprise has made his own company, with 8,000 employees in the Bavarian town of Selb, one of Germany's most successful examples of industrial democracy.

In this case-study Philip Rosenthal explains the evolution of worker participation in his company, and gives his personal views on its essential role in the process of leadership and communication.

We Germans may be more inclined than others to underrate what we have and what we ourselves have achieved, be it in economic wealth or political reform. Those of us who travel abroad know how well the Bundesrepublik is admired because we have found the 'third way', the middle course between unlimited capitalism and bureaucratic communism – workers participating in private industry in both 'saying' (co-determination) and 'having' (capital-sharing). If we Germans, and particularly Rosenthal AG, have weathered the recent crisis better than other countries it is at least in part because worker participation has averted the extreme confrontation that is so detrimental to everyone.

As chairman and chief executive of a company confronted with co-determination, I opposed it for a long time. I made no secret of it either, despite the fact that I was already a Social Democratic Member of Parliament. At the time my reasons were the usual ones – it obstructs or at least delays necessary management decisions, and it exerts a political influence in the board room.

I eventually changed my mind. The overriding reason for this was practical experience.

1. *Each social group, be it a country, a political party, a club or a family, can remain stable only when the majority view predominates.*

Even in the purely political field the democratic ideal of citizens making all political decisions can never be a reality. But citizens ultimately decide by whom they are represented. Further, they have the opportunity to remove and replace their representatives. This kind of participation is a crucial factor in creating and maintaining stability and is an undervalued factor compared, for example, with wealth of which we can never get enough and which is overvalued. An obvious example of this simple truth is the blacks in South Africa and Rhodesia. Their standard of living is considerably higher than that in black African countries, yet participation does not exist for them as it does for others in the same country, and their situation as a result remains highly explosive.

2. *Life at work for the worker is more important than politics, and in most cases just as important as life outside work.*

It is only when a worker feels that he is a part of and a party to decisions in his company that he will identify personally with the issues and events affecting the company. Otherwise there remains the feeling that decisions are simply taken by 'those up there'.

Thus, co-determination has a double function of positive influence. First, the worker knows that he is participating. Second, he knows and understands the company's needs. It also has a positive impact on the attitudes and actions of trade unions. In industrial countries trade unions have found themselves torn between either making selfish wage claims, backed with the threat of strikes (leading to the dreadful results of inflation and/or decreased investments, as in Italy and Britain), or considering the economic success of industry as a part of their own. If they participate in the choice between necessary investments and financing research or expansion, or squandering company profits on inflationary wage rates, holiday bonuses and the avoidance of unpopular rationalization, the trade unionist will act differently and more responsibly than he would if he is required to perform his task in a mood of confrontation. It is no accident that co-determination is anathema not only to reactionary business leaders but also to revolutionaries who consider class struggle a means to eliminate private property in the economic system.

The potential disadvantages of co-determination (at least of the type we have opted for in Germany) pale against such factors as these. Yet they cannot be ignored. The chief concern must be the effects on management's ability not only to take decisions, but to take decisions in time. There remains the possibility, in theory at least, that necessary decisions can be blocked or delayed. This might be especially true of the German coal and steel industry, which has had parity worker representation on the supervisory board since the last war. But experience has proved that key decisions have not been obstructed by parity – indeed, the co-operation of workers has ensured that they are carried out without confrontation or conflict. This is not just my personal opinion, incidentally, but that of a committee under the guidance of Professor Biedenkopf, the former general secretary of the conservative opposition party.

The novelty of the German model is that the workers' delegation on the supervisory board includes proportional representation for middle management as well as shopfloor workers. This is a truer form of industrial democracy because it corresponds to the structure of the employees. Middle management delegates in most cases contribute additional knowledge and understanding of the company's needs. They are nominated by their colleagues but elected by all employees. The result is balanced and acceptable representation and the avoidance of any suggestion that they necessarily support the stockholders' interests.

Excessive trade union influence is avoided in the German model by allowing only one-third of the workers' delegation to be drawn from trade unionists not employed by the company – and even these are selected by an employee vote. These outsiders correspond logically to bankers representing stockholder interests on the supervisory board.

At Rosenthal AG we have not been pioneers in co-determination. We have merely filled existing laws willingly with life. And in anticipation of forthcoming legislation, a woman delegate of the workers has been elected to the presidential committee of the supervisory board. Where we have been pioneers, however, is in the area of capital-sharing. We have done this not only because social justice demands it, but because joint ownership leads to a more intensified joint understanding.

It is also an economic necessity. To prove the point let us take the simple example of a company that has sales of DM10 million, costs of DM9 million, thus leaving a profit of DM1 million. In today's economic context this company has four alternatives.

1. Remain competitive and highly profitable by ploughing this year's profit back into new plant and machinery and perhaps investing some in humanizing the work environment, leaving little for increased wages. This is not only unfair, but is unrealistic and unacceptable to the trade unions.

2. Use virtually all the profit to increase wages at the expense of investment, expansion or rationalization. This leads inevitably to reduced competitiveness and ultimately to unemployment (Britain is an example and warning of this to us all).

3. Use virtually all profit to increase wages; funds needed for new investments will be provided by increasing prices. This is the most frequent compromise, the short-term easy way out that leads inevitably to inflation and complaints from workers that their wage increases are worthless.

4. Accept that investments must be made to safeguard the future, and that some new way must be found to ensure that workers participate in the long-term growth and wealth that will result from those investments. The only alternative to the untenable situation of capital concentration with a minority is for workers to participate in the capital of our economy.

The realization that this fourth alternative is the only valid one for the future of our economic system is no longer confined to any one political party. It is an accepted responsibility for the reasoned centre, the far-sighted, in all parties, the trade unions and industry.

It was the early realization of these social and political facts that caused us at Rosenthal to start our own capital-sharing model in 1963.

Instead of a profit-sharing cash bonus, we agreed after discussion with the workers' council to introduce a long-term saving programme through capital-sharing. The first step was to give each employee one Rosenthal share. Starting in 1967 each employee who had been working for the company longer than five years received a grant of DM156 to assist his purchase of additional company shares. This enabled us to encourage capital formation for our younger employees. As a result, in 1967 our employees owned 5 per cent of the Rosenthal AG share capital.

Realizing that there is a natural limit to the amount that workers will invest in their own company, we introduced new schemes from 1968 to 1970 giving our employees investment shares in existing funds, in addition to the original scheme offering them Rosenthal stock. From 1971 to 1973 additional purchases of company stock and investment certificates were encouraged by company subsidies ranging from 10 to 20 per cent, depending upon the number of shares or certificates bought. The number of employees participating in the scheme increased greatly: 6 per cent in 1965, 20 per cent in 1967, and now more than 50 per cent.

Our model for capital-sharing has also helped other companies, including those that cannot hand out shares owing to their legal structure, to develop schemes enabling their workers to acquire productive capital.

But our model was not without its faults. Stock exchange losses and the international economic crisis lead to a loss of confidence and a reluctance to continue to invest in productive capital. Such schemes need continual adjustments and improvements. (This is the thrust behind our new scheme, 'Aktion '77'.) However, including investment certificates, our employees now own some DM9 million productive capital, the equivalent of 15 per cent of the stock value of our company.

To me, capital sharing is a logical development of co-determination in creating an effective and stable industrial democracy. But industrial democracy is a very demanding middle course between traditional capitalism and bureaucratic communism. For a start, it requires a quality of management leadership and management skills that the other two systems have little use for. Management in many countries resists the process towards the participative form of industrial democracy because they doubt the ability of their workers to grasp the economic essentials of private industry and their willingness to contribute to the process. I wonder whether, in reality, it is not more that they doubt the ability of management to explain the economic essentials in terms that will be relevant and acceptable to their workers.

Stable industrial democracy results from and depends upon effective communication among all the parties involved to achieve a common understanding of the objectives being pursued. Communication and a will to make the system work (the latter resulting largely from the former) are the twin instruments of its success. The German model has established a framework within which effective communication is possible. To the legal framework must be added such communication forums as workers' and company councils, and the two-tier board with all 'participants' having a voice on the supervisory board that sets policy. Management has learnt that communication leading to understanding is not a question of giving orders. Workers and the trade unions know that it is not simply a question of making demands. There is no place for confrontation in effective communication – it is a process of give and take, and of wanting to understand the interests and point of view of other participants in the system.

In Germany, as in a handful of other countries, we have begun to master this art of communication because we have realized that the will to communicate, the first essential, must be matched by the ability to communicate. All participants have learnt now not only the need to listen but also the need to express their viewpoint in a way that is intelligible to the others.

Voltaire used to read everything he wrote to his cook. If she could not understand it he used to rewrite it. There is a lesson here for all participants in industrial democracy, management not least.

18

Communication and Crisis

It may take years for a company to earn and build a good reputation. It can take a day of mishandled crisis to destroy it. Gulf Oil recognized this, and did something about it.

In this case-study Jayne Baker Spain, a senior vice-president of Gulf Oil Corporation, outlines the disaster communication training programme that her company developed with outside public relations counsel. More than 2,000 Gulf managers around the world have participated in the programme and are subject to a new company policy making communication with the public the responsibility of every manager.

For the distinguished Gulf manager, holder of a number of patents, author of several technical papers, his assignment must not have seemed too difficult. He was to appear, that warm spring evening in the early 1970s, before a public hearing of the State Air Quality Control Board; his purpose, to outline the significant progress Gulf's local plant was making in complying with the state's newly enacted air-pollution control law.

He would also request a variance, i.e. a delay in the enforcement of the law affecting the Gulf facility. In the manager's mind, such a delay was justified. The project involved major construction and many millions of dollars to eliminate certain emissions at the plant. These emissions, mainly dust, had been tolerated by the community for years, constituting more of a nuisance than any serious threat.

The mayor of the surrounding community in which Gulf was a major employer, the head of the local air quality board, and other community leaders would testify on Gulf's behalf and in favour of the variance.

The hearing examiners were, the manager knew, not politicians or even experts in the field, but university graduate students retained temporarily by the state for this assignment.

There would be some opponents in the audience – environmental activists – but then their group was small and not technically competent. The manager had a great deal of difficulty understanding them, his knowledge limited to news reports of their often-outrageous statements. Also attending would be some reporters from the local and state press, but the manager had instructed his public relations representative to prepare a release for them, summarizing the testimony he was about to give, and the release had been approved by headquarters – after a two-week wait – that afternoon.

Now as the hearings began, with the fresh-faced hearing examiners seated high behind the judge's bench of the old city courtroom and the Gulf manager standing behind the wooden gate of the witnesses' dock below, he was invited to deliver his opening statement.

Assisted by his charts and graphs, he did so with some pride, outlining the months of engineering work, the difficulty of applying a new technology, and pointing out that Gulf had put the whole programme on a crash basis in order to comply as quickly as possible. He showed photographs of the site preparation work already in progress and showed copies of contracts for the new pollution control equipment that the company had ordered.

He explained, however, that there had been some delays – that was normal when dealing with new technology. And in fact, he had received that day – and here he pulled the telegram from his pocket – notification from one manufacturer that a vital piece of equipment could not be delivered on schedule. The manager said he was very concerned about this development, and he intended to fly to the manufacturer's plant the very next day to see what could be done to expedite the delivery – here he waved his airline ticket for the examiners to see.

'Mr. _____,' roared the youthful hearing examiner, "the people of the State of _____ have heard enough of your lies!'

Two and a half hours later, stunned into silence by shouted accusations, humiliated repeatedly, his competence questioned, his motives impugned, his carefully reasoned technical arguments dismissed or ignored, the manager was permitted to step down to face a now thoroughly aroused and hostile press.

'Was it true that Gulf was trying to evade the law?'

'Didn't Gulf care what effect this pollution might be having on school children?'

'Wasn't it true that Gulf favoured clean air only so long as it didn't cost any money?'

The manager never did make the trip to the manufacturer's plant the next day. He went home that night too ill from the experience.

A few weeks later – after the uproar had subsided – Gulf's request for an air quality variance could have been denied, or routinely granted. But relations with the community and certain community leaders who were embarrassed on that occasion would be long in healing. As for the manager, his competence is questioned; his confidence and, perhaps, his health is permanently weakened.

This case is a consolidation of a series of such incidents, many of them occurring in the late 1960s and early 1970s, as large American corporations – and particularly oil companies – became the targets of the general anger and social unrest which swept the U.S.A. Other institutions came under duress during the period, but Business – narrow, parochial, unaccustomed to self-examination – was perhaps less well prepared.

Within the space of a few short years, oil companies were forced to cope with stringent new environmental regulations, government-imposed minority-hiring policies, a price freeze, war-stimulated inflation and declining profitability. They were required to deal with the costly and difficult problem of removing lead from gasoline. Reserves were declining at home, and business relationships abroad becoming increasingly unstable.

Society demanded change and demanded it immediately. In the impatient and uneasy climate of the times, any delays, any counter-proposals were interpreted as back-sliding or irresponsible, or worse. There were bomb threats, mass picketing and angry demonstrations. Gulf managers found themselves involved in frequent confrontations.

The need, of course, was to communicate. We had things to say, many of which might have contributed to the more rapid realization of the goals that society now wished to achieve. But in the area of communications, the industry was simply not prepared to cope.

For years, oil companies had enjoyed a relatively untroubled relationship with the American public. Prices were low; price wars frequent, so that the consumer got a bargain routinely; retail marketing contests, prizes and give-aways. Stock prices soared with the rest of the early 1960s, along with profits and dividends. There was little need to explain the industry's problems to the public – it didn't seem to have many. Besides, the industry was complicated and technical, difficult for the layman to understand, and there were national security aspects to the business, another reason for limiting communications.

At Gulf, company policy dictated that any communications with the press be cleared through the corporate secretary, a process which, at the minimum, required several days. As problems intensified, however, this policy became an 'Achilles Heel'.

Faced with picketing, protests and a suddenly interested and unsympathetic press, Gulf managers either said nothing at all (strictly observing company policy) or reflected it, in effect believing it wasn't any of the public's business, which contributed to suspicions and hostilities between 'them' and 'us'. Even senior managers, unused to dealing with reporters and unsure of how much they could say, missed frequent opportunities to explain misconceptions about the industry or to contribute to public understanding of problems.

Operating managers were at a particular disadvantage. Isolated in their local communities and not authorized to discuss company policy, they found themselves besieged by environmentalists, social activists, consumer protectionists and other special interest groups.

As early as 1970, Gulf began searching for a programme to make managers more skilful in dealing with public issues. The company sought the advice of Burson-Marsteller, a public relations consulting firm which had designed a disaster communications training programme for another company.

Burson-Marsteller and Gulf's public relations department took a year to research Gulf problems and devise a training programme of sufficient realism. It was recognized at once that managers couldn't simply be called in and lectured; some way had to be found to enlist their co-operation, to convince them of the importance of community relations, and to assure them that – should they venture forth into the perilous area of public communications – their jobs wouldn't be in jeopardy if they said the wrong thing. Most importantly, it was recognized that managers who had experienced a public relations crisis were sensitized by the experience and active believers in maintaining effective community relations.

The result was 'Crisisport', a day-long, intensive seminar which confronts managers with a variety of simulated and dramatized community crises. In a day in which 'everything that can go wrong, does', a hostile community attacks the managers with labour demands, civil rights criticism, consumer complaints and environmental restrictions. As though that isn't enough, the day ends with a refinery explosion. Film, slides, television and radio are used to dramatize the incidents. Professional actors play some of the roles of activist opponents.

Throughout the day, the managers are required to participate vigorously. They are called upon to answer angry telephone calls, talk to inquiring news reporters, meet with activists and government officials and face an angry public hearing like the one opening this chapter. They are required to communicate, to explain Gulf policies and defend Gulf actions as best they can, frequently to hostile and unbelieving adversaries.

The programme began in San Diego in 1972 and has since been presented for more than 1,300 Gulf managers in the United States, plus others in Europe and Latin America. Managers attended in groups of fifty to sixty, carefully selected for a mix of responsibilities and expertise. Bosses and subordinates were kept out of the same sessions.

Changes were made to adapt the programme to local conditions overseas. In Latin America (where the entire programme was done in Spanish) student nationals were substituted for the black activists used in the US version; their demands were altered to represent, as realistically as possible, the demands of activists in the particular country in which the programme was presented.

In Europe the differences in employee–management relations and consumer relations had to be taken into account, and, as much as possible, the problems adapted to local cultural and political traditions.

At first there were some problems. Managers complained they were being told to communicate with the public when their policy manuals told them they could do no such thing. 'You expect me to answer a reporter on the spot,' one manager remarked, 'when you know it would take me two or three weeks to get approval to do that.' Other managers translated the policy to mean that, while the company trusted them to run operations worth hundreds of millions of dollars, they were not trusted, apparently, to explain those operations to a reporter.

The result was a prompt and significant policy change which now gives Gulf managers much greater freedom – indeed, responsibility – to communicate with the public. A new fifty-page communications manual has been issued with news interview tips such as: never say 'no comment' to a journalist; don't be coy or evasive; if you don't know the answer, say, 'I don't know', then make every effort to supply the information. Follow-up special training for television interviews are necessary.

The objectives of the programme are to make managers, first of all, more aware of their responsibilities in community and public relations. Managers, after all, represent Gulf in their local communities; they are

expected to be able to explain the company's actions. Secondly, the programme aims to give managers a crash course in how to deal with those
responsibilities: how to talk to the press, for example, and how to respond
to and, hopefully, soften hostility. Finally, the programme serves as a
vehicle to communicate policy, offering as it does a day-long discussion of
industry problems and how the company regards them.

A day in 'Crisisport' (a mythical community which has a variety of
Gulf installations) begins with an introduction to that community.
Managers are told the size and population; they are briefed on the local
economy and local politics. They are even given brief biographical
sketches of influential citizens, such as a friendly mayor and an unfriendly
local journalist and city councilman.

Problems begin with some unpleasant phone calls from local
customers and residents, then the arrival of the local morning paper, the
Crisisport Post. Five different editions are distributed, each headlining a
contentious problem involving Gulf. In one case rumour has it that Gulf
will lay off some refinery workers; in another environmentalists have
moved to block a Gulf application to drill for oil offshore; in yet another
Gulf is criticized for opposing a local transportation referendum. In each
case, the newspaper accounts are distorted – at least in part because the
local Gulf manager has failed to be properly responsive with the press.

The managers are separated into five teams and told to deal with the
problems. Each team is given the real facts in its case, and is asked to come
up with two answers:

1. what do you do now, to deal with this problem?
2. how could you – if you were the local manager – have prevented this
   from happening?

After some time to discuss the problems, the teams are reconvened
and asked to present their solutions. The responses are criticized by the
rest of the audience during a typically lively discussion of staff specialists
who help guide the discussion and emphasize that there are no 'right'
answers to many complex community relations situations, but that
managers are expected to be aware of what's going on in their
communities. They are expected to anticipate unfavourable public
reaction to company actions, to avoid it where possible and to plan ahead
to deal with it when it does occur. The headlined cases are designed to
leave the managers with the impression that it is far more desirable to
prevent a problem than to have to solve it once it has reached page one.

As the day progresses, the managers are required to represent Gulf in
ever more difficult situations. They receive phone calls from irate citizens;

they are required to meet with a hostile civil rights pressure group on employment discrimination; they must attend a city council hearing to defend the company against charges of polluting the local environment, and finally, they must assume command in a simulated refinery disaster.

Even lunch affords no break in the pressure. Invited speakers are real industry critics, many of whom took the opportunity to excoriate the managers for the past Gulf actions or policies.

The final exercise of the day is the refinery disaster, which is a lesson in crisis management as well as community and public relations. A filmed 'TV News' report of the disaster lends authenticity to the exercise. The managers are required to deal with the situation as if it were real: to make decisions to protect lives, contain the fire and limit the damage, as well as to cope with a host of impatient newsmen pushing for the cause of the blaze, names of the missing or dead and other difficult questions.

Complicating the manager's role is the fact that he receives information only the way he would receive it in a real emergency, i.e. from incomplete reports and differing points of view. As in real-life situations, some of the information is just not right, so that the manager has the additional problem of deciding whether what he knows is true.

At the conclusion of the exercise, the manager's actions are criticized by a panel of newspaper and broadcast journalists who explained- sometimes not too tactfully – that if their photographers and film camera teams weren't permitted to approach the scene of an emergency, they would sneak over the fence or smuggle themselves into the plant in the back of emergency vehicles. And if the manager wouldn't grant an interview, then their talk with the guard at the gate, and other imperfect observers, would be the sole sources of the news they could find.

Benefits of the programmes to Gulf have been immediate and gratifying. One pleasant surprise was that many managers could cope quite well with the problems; they knew the answers without prompting from the public relations, labour relations or personnel staff experts. In fact, in the first seminars, when such experts were given a more active role as participants, the managers resented it. They proved that they were aware of many of their difficulties and – given the authority – they knew what to do about them.

Another advantage was that, with managers assuming their proper role as the local community official of the company, public relations people were relieved of that duty, for which they have the least credibility.

Some of the best results:

1. The manager of a credit card operation, who found he could not hire black applicants because of a lack of more direct public transportation

to his suburban location, was able to persuade the bus company to extend service. The result of this excellent public example has added jobs and goodwill in his community, as well as a means of meeting his goal in hiring minorities.

2. Marketing managers were assigned the unhappy task of eliminating unprofitable dealerships, raising dealer rents and making other unpopular adjustments to the system that had provoked angry public and dealer reaction in the past. This time, the managers were told they were responsible for any adverse community reaction as well. It was their job to accomplish this with minimum dealer reaction, and to explain why it was reasonable for Gulf to do these things and why they were, ultimately, in the best interests of both the dealers and the consumer. The result – unlike previous occasions – was virtually no bad publicity for Gulf.

3. A crisis-trained coal mine manager was able to avert a shutdown of the mine when, following an accident, his quick, accurate communications prevented false rumours of unsafe mine conditions from gaining credence.

4. A refinery manager was able to avert a public panic when early news reports suggested that a refinery fire might endanger homes of nearby residents.

5. A large number of Gulf managers were ready to help explain to their communities the energy crisis brought on by the Arab oil embargo.

In 1975, a second 'Crisisport' was devised, based on the success of the first. 'Bunker Point', as the new programme was called, was specifically designed to help managers deal with the problems of oil spills. Burson-Marsteller and Gulf's public relations department again combined to research and develop the seminar, which has now been presented to some 700 Gulf ship's officers and managers of refineries, storage tank terminals and other bulk oil-handling facilities in the United States, Canada, Puerto Rico, Ireland and England. The specific goals of the programme were to re-emphasize to managers the serious and costly consequences of oil spills, to introduce Gulf's latest spill-prevention programme and policies, and to train the managers to handle both the spills and public communications about such incidents.

Many of the same techniques are employed, including audio-visual dramatizations, role-playing, simulated interviews with newspeople and some training in dealing with the press.

The highlight of the day is a simulated meeting with government officials in the midst of a massive oil spill. The managers are forced to deal with an angry environmentalist, a local politician who feels threatened by Gulf's disaster, and, simultaneously, a minister of the national government who is making a direct report to the country's president.

Panels of experts in marine operations, terminal management, environmental and public affairs debate the problems with the managers as they arise and offer their advice.

Some of the immediate benefits of this programme include a decline in both the number and severity of oil spills occurring at Gulf installations or involving Gulf vessels, and an increase in the reporting of minor spills, with more careful analysis of why and how those spills happened.

Both 'Crisisport' and 'Bunker Point' were highly rated by the managers who attended. Both programmes were awarded the 'Silver Anvil', highest national award of the Public Relations Society of United States, and both have been widely and favourably reported in the business press. 'Bunker Point' so impressed observers from other companies that Gulf was asked to do an additional session of the programme for managers of other American and Canadian oil corporations.

Perhaps the most important lesson of both seminars is that in today's world business decisions must be made with a regard for and appreciation of public opinion, and that the best way for those business decisions to be understood by the public is to have them communicated directly by the decision-makers themselves.

19

The Nuclear Debate

The future of nuclear energy, which has been the subject of public debate in virtually all Western countries, is an emotional as well as an economic and scientific issue. It has aroused angry and often irrational argument from both sides, and in some countries violent demonstration. In the Netherlands the debate has taken a different course. There, emotion and rhetoric have been tempered by the activities of a group of individuals who set out to achieve two things: considerable delay in the decision on nuclear policy, and an assurance that the decision would be taken only after full consideration of the hazards and alternatives.

It became known as the Reflection Group. In this case-study its founder and co-ordinator, Eric-Jan Tuininga, describes how it used communication techniques to succeed in both its objectives, and what it learned about influencing government policy.

Eric-Jan Tuininga is a Dutch mechanical engineer with American and European business experience. He now works in the non-profit sector.

In late 1974 private discussion on the expansion of nuclear power in the Netherlands became an intensive public debate. There were two causes: first, several thousands of Dutch citizens refused to continue paying a 3 per cent levy on their electricity bills to fund a multinational project for an experimental fast-breeder reactor. Second, a long-overdue government policy paper on energy was leaked and revealed plans for a substantial expansion of nuclear power production during the next ten years through the construction of three massive nuclear plants.

Unimpressed by the arguments used to justify this expansion, a group of twenty-three concerned individuals sat down together and prepared a paper of their own on nuclear energy policy in the Netherlands. The group included journalists, Members of Parliament from four government parties and several scientists, including some from industry. In their paper they asked for a five-year 'period of reflection' before any more commerical power plants were built.

The group did not present itself as anti-nuclear. Its only concern was the quality of the government's arguments for taking what seemed to be a hasty decision on the expansion of nuclear power in such a densely populated country.

The Reflection Group, as it became known, in fact comprised individuals with many different views on the use of nuclear power; but they shared a concern about the lack of thorough analysis by government of all the energy options, and about the shallowness of information on the subject given to Parliament in particular.

Initially the Group's strategy was to upgrade the public debate on energy. This was achieved in part through publication of the Group's first 'reflection paper' on nuclear energy policy. But the Group knew there was need for a continued flow of independent information on energy matters until Parliament took a formal decision on the government's proposed plans.

One of the most serious shortcomings the Group saw in the government paper was that it gave only token treatment to social, ecological and political factors. A second shortcoming was that possible alternatives for energy production (coal for the middle term and alternative sources for the long term) were treated rather scornfully, whereas the possible, probable and even empirically known disadvantages of nuclear power were essentially ignored. That strong and influential groups had played a large part in producing this distorted picture is suggested by the fact that an earlier version of the energy paper prepared by the Ministry of Economic Affairs (though arriving at the same conclusions as the final report) discussed the disadvantages of nuclear power in some detail. This report was leaked out. Apparently it was decided at a higher level that such treatment would have a negative effect on 'doubt removal' and that these things should be left unsaid.

Just before the government energy policy paper was discussed in the Council of Ministers, the first 'reflection paper' by the Group was presented at a press conference. It also carried the support of thirty-three important scientists and leading theologians (both Protestant and Catholic). These were included to emphasize the ethical aspects of the introduction of nuclear power, and also to influence the ministers and politicians from two religious parties in the government coalition.

The paper made headlines, and the publication of the government energy paper was postponed several weeks. Once published it indicated a compromise. No longer were the three proposed nuclear plants definite. There was a decision in principle to have them operating in 1985, however, subject to completion of several studies on health, safety and siting aspects.

The promised studies were published within a year and by the end of 1975 the Dutch Minister of Economic Affairs concluded that the way was clear for the expansion of nuclear power.

Again, just before the Council of Ministers was to decide on the issue, a second 'reflection paper' was published by the Group. This paper was an attempt to make a socio-economic quantification of nuclear power and the alternative options in the light of new forecasts up to 1985. The Reflection Group concluded once more that no decision was necessary on nuclear expansion as other options had not been carefully analysed.

The government, under political pressure from a threatening internal crisis, decided to postpone the decision. It was explained that an immediate decision was no longer necessary because the energy situation was not as bad as it originally seemed. Thus, it was argued, the three nuclear power stations would be needed not by 1985, but later.

However, Parliament still had to approve this decision, and the Reflection Group sponsored a third 'reflection paper' on the possibility of decentralization of electricity generation. Additionally, an abstract of the second 'reflection paper' was prepared as a full-page advertisement published in leading Dutch newspapers. This advertisement was paid for and signed by 1,200 concerned scientists, business leaders, a Nobel laureat, leading theologians and a former president of the European Commission.

In February 1976 Parliament approved the postponement of the decision on the nuclear programme until after the elections of spring 1977. So, from the start of the Reflection Group's activities in 1974, a three-year 'period of reflection' had already been secured.

Since the decision the Reflection Group has helped to keep the nuclear debate alive by publishing papers and exerting pressure on the government on such issues as proposed Dutch involvement in a French fast-breeder programme, and a uranium enrichment plant in the Netherlands.

The strategy of the Group has always been primarily to produce unbiased information by publishing papers and statements which were sent to national decision-makers, ministers, and Members of Parliament. By calling frequent press conferences, new information was given maximum coverage in the media. Once the role of the group as an independent source of information was acknowledged by most interested parties, more informal meetings were arranged with politicians, industrialists, trade union leaders and government officials.

As more people demanded the papers of the group, the problem of organization arose. Some members decided to start a foundation, 'Energy and Society', which was set up together with an environmental organization related to Friends of the Earth. This foundation made it possible to reproduce the papers and send them to a wide range of individuals beyond decision-makers at national level who had until then been the group's primary target. The foundation, which acts as home base for the Reflection Group, began publishing a monthly newsletter in 1975 aimed at opinion leaders in the energy field in government, industry and the media. The newsletter is sent free of charge and consists of twelve pages of abstracts of articles from all over the world on the social and economic implications of energy developments. The low cost of the newsletter is met by contributions from group members and others, and in 1976 it was granted a small subsidy by the Ministry of Science.

In 1974 the Reflection Group faced strong opposition. The pro-nuclear lobby was well entrenched after some fifteen years of government support for nuclear projects. But it was evidently uneasy about the composition of the Group and the fact that it included a number of high-level industrial scientists. Initially the pro-nuclear lobby claimed that the call for a period of reflection was simply strategy, and that the real aim of the Group was a ban on nuclear energy in the Netherlands.

The Reflection Group had stepped into a polarized discussion on nuclear energy and established itself as an independent *ad hoc* think tank on energy matters. Most of its members were considered to be respectable scientists or politicians and could acceptably communicate with opposing parties in the nuclear debate. Several members started a discussion with people from the nuclear industry which resulted in a mutual publication on the choice between coal and nuclear energy for electricity generation.

Other members felt more at ease with trade union specialists and talked to them about the unions' energy policy, also questioning the use of nuclear energy.

On the many discussion platforms on energy matters Group members got to know government officials responsible for energy planning which resulted in mutual brainstorming sessions on energy conservation policy. Through their membership of the Reflection Group many of them were invited to join policy-making sessions at many levels. Virtually all political parties, churches and professional organizations in Holland have discussion or advisory groups on energy. Diffusion of the Reflection Group's ideas has vastly increased through these institutions.

The pro-nuclear lobby soon discovered that the arguments of the Reflection Group could not be dismissed in the same way it had discounted those of many anti-nuclear groups. It had characterized these as being irresponsible, inexpert and politically naive. As a result the pro-nuclear lobby tried a different tactic with the Reflection Group. It ignored it.

However, as soon as it became clear that government thinking on nuclear energy was changing, the pro-nuclear lobby was forced to react differently. It began a vigorous campaign, commenting on papers published by the Reflection Group. It even produced a regular newsletter of its own. But this strategy failed too. The pro-nuclear lobby found itself operating in a strange and new environment. It had to negotiate with a less sympathetic Council of Ministers; it faced growing opposition in Parliament and among the general public; and it faced the Reflection Group, which had gained considerable credibility and influence. So again the pro-nuclear lobby changed its strategy and concentrated most of its efforts on government officials known to be sympathetic to its cause. By that time, however, it was too late to prevent postponement of government plans until after the 1977 elections.

The experience of the Reflection Group shows that the main weakness of national decision-making on major technological developments is the lack of credible information on all possible alternative options.

Until recently, government could get away with choosing a certain option and sending stacks of preselected, supporting evidence to convince Parliament. As in many other countries, the argument in Holland was: 'We've spent billions on this nuclear development already, so we better start using it.'

The key lesson from the Dutch experience is that, not only should information for decision-making be relevant and understandable for non-experts, but it should also be presented as objectively as possible, by credible people, to the real decision-makers at the right time. This sounds like textbook advice, so let's take a closer look at these issues.

Objectivity can greatly be improved by a comparison of several alternative options and an assessment of as many of the possible consequences of each of these. Objectivity can be greatly improved by admitting negative aspects of one's own favoured solution. For instance, the first 'reflection paper' might have been stronger by admitting some negative aspects of the suggested five-year reflection period.

Credibility depends on the level of people that support the information. Just taking one Nobel Laureate does not enhance credibility *per se;* it takes balance of argument as well as of people.

The real decision-makers in the short run on the issue of technological developments are mostly government ministers and Parliament. In the middle term decisions are taken by the planners in industry and government, and for the long term by the general public. The Reflection Group chose to work for short-term results and consequently aimed at the first target group. But as the objective of postponement of the nuclear decision was met, the group automatically had to give more attention to the planners.

At the right time is a last and very important criteria for communication success. All the Reflection Group really did was put together the most recent information on a certain energy matter and deliver it to the top decision-makers at the moment they had to start thinking about it. Often the best information given too early is worse than reasonable information delivered at the right time. Decision-makers in industry and government always lack time to read through their papers and correspondence.

Public decision-makers nowadays have too many lobbyists knocking at their doors advocating some issue or option. But they have hardly any source of timely and reliable information on all the alternative options and their consequences. The Reflection Group bridged this gap.

20

A Takeover

One of the longest and most fascinating takeover tussles in British commercial history was the battle over Shipping Industrial Holdings (SIH). It began in 1972 and ended over a year later. The final outcome was perhaps inevitable, but the spirited defence put up by the SIH board dragged the fight out and pushed up the price that the bidding consortium had to pay for it to a remarkably high level. In this case-study Brian Basham, now a financial PR consultant but at the time a financial journalist with The Times, describes how the SIH board used every available communication trump card in the deck to achieve this objective.

As an industrialist, the career of Mr Peter Parker, now chairman of British Rail, was plagued by predators and by 1973 he had twice clashed with asset stripper supreme Jim Slater.

In round one Parker had lost control of Associated British Maltsters after Slater had built up a stake and sold it on to Dalgety, but in round two he had foiled the financier's plans for the acquisition of glass manufacturers Rockware, after Slater had quietly acquired a 25 per cent holding.

At the end of 1973 Peter Parker emerged from yet another fight again involving Slater. It was one of the longest takeover tussles in British

commercial history: the fight for control of Shipping Industrial Holdings.
The battle holds a special place in the memories of takeover
afficionados because of the explosive emotions it aroused, the reputations it
tarnished and the skill of the defensive in-fighting. The SIH board's
defence against odds that eventually overwhelmed them, but at a price,
was a classic, and their strategies and tactics, their organization and liaison,
the forces they marshalled and the audiences they communicated with are
a worthy study for any manager who fears that his company too may one
day attract the attention of an unwelcome suiter – from the private or state
sectors.

Like so many of those companies that attract the attentions of the
asset-strippers in the late 1960s and early 1970s, SIH was chock-full of
assets but its share price was temporarily depressed. The fall in its share
price had been caused by the collapse of its tour operation subsidiary,
Clarksons, in 1971 and 1972, despite the success of its other activities as
shipbrokers, insurance brokers and shipowners.

From the beginning, Clarkson Tours had made an important
contribution to SIH Group profits; £228,000 out of a group total of
£961,000 in 1967; £335,000 out of £1.4 million in 1968; £418,000 of £1.7
million in 1969; £447,000 of £4.3 million in 1970.

And then disaster!

From being a useful contributor with profits in a good year two-thirds
the size of the biggest single contributor (still shipbroking), Tours turned
into a millstone which threatened to drown the company: in 1971 a loss of
£2.7 million against profits for the rest of the group of £4.8 million; and in
1972 a loss of £4.8 million against the rest of the Group's £5.5 million.

News of the troubles of the Tours company sent SIH shares
plummeting until the whole group was valued in the market at less than
£28.5 million with the shares at 168p, the lowest level since 1968 and
down from their 1971 peak of 368p.

Signs of a burgeoning interest were not long in coming. By October
1972 the *Daily Express* was reporting that 600,000 shares had changed
hands in one day and the shares rose to 252p. By the end of the year the
shares were up to 280p, and at that point Peter Parker took over as
chairman of Clarkson Tours (he was by then also deputy chairman of SIH)
on the condition that among his options he could be free to sell Clarksons.

A series of crucial events then took place in rapid succession. The first
real warnings of the presence of a predator came in an article in *The Times*
on the last day of February 1973 when reporter Maurice Barnfather
secured for himself a minor scoop with the story that stakes of around 6 per
cent had been accumulated in SIH by a company by the name of Doddel

Limited, which had been registered the previous year with a share capital of just £100. The real owners remained a mystery. With memories of Associated British Maltsters and Rockware fresh in his mind Parker had a distinct impression of a *déjà vu.*

Within days his worst fears were voiced when on 13 March the London *Evening Standard* reported stock market rumours that a second-line City finance house, Triumph Investment Trust, had sold 'a large chunk of shares' to none other than Slater Walker.

At the end of April, SIH finally rid itself of its incubus by selling 85 per cent to Court Line for the nominal sum of £1. The SIH shares leaped in the market despite the fact that the company had been forced to back the deal with a £5.7 million payment to cover against the Tour operators' losses in the current year. It was in fact a very good deal for SIH. Just a month earlier Thomson, it was reported, had demanded £10 million to take Clarksons on.

With benefit of 20/20 hindsight, Jocelyn Hambro, in his last statement as chairman of the SIH Group, described the board's reasons for disposing of the company in the following words:

> Your board decided that a massive involvement in this entirely new consumer type industry was not complementary to our strengths in the shipping and insurance businesses. The logical home for sound development of the Holidays company was with its main airline carrier, Court Line Limited . . . . In this integration lies a real future for Clarksons Holidays and for the people in the company who sustained it through this critical period.

Court Line went into liquidation in August 1974.

Confirmation of Slater's involvement in SIH came in May, when he revealed his hand by selling a 12½ per cent stake which he had built up over a period of three months to none other than Hambros, SIH's own merchant bank and the 'family firm' of Jocelyn Hambro. Slater was reputed to have made a £1 million dealing profit in the process.

Hambros's move pulled the rug out from under the SIH board. Only a few days before SIH managing director Mr David Gault had been confidently telling the press that between SIH directors and Hambros they could muster 30 per cent support against an unwelcome bidder. Now, they felt, Hambros's allegiance could not be counted on and the SIH directors were aware of the bank's strong connections with the Norwegian shipowner Hilmar Reksten, who, despite his age (seventy-six), still maintained grandiose plans for the restructuring of the shipping industry. Moreover, in his own right he had been a founding 10 per cent shareholder in SIH. All sorts of convoluted possibilities were in the minds of the directors and for a while the most likely seemed the suggestion that Hambros was willing to hand up SIH on a plate to the P & O shipping line on the condition that P & O dropped its efforts to gain control of its US shipping partner, Zapata Ness, which Hilmar Reksten himself was at that time also fighting for.

It came as a further shock when, at the end of May, the board suddenly learnt that Hambros had approached the City Takeover Panel to inquire whether it could buy up on special premium terms a further 10 per cent stake without being obliged to bid for the outstanding equity. The stake was held by another well-known market dealer, Mr Jimmy Goldsmith, who was also a Hambros client.

That move destroyed the last vestige of trust between the bank and its former client. Parker went round to the Takeover Panel like a shot, complaining that he believed that there had been fiduciary abuse of the relationship between merchant banker and client.

Hambros did not eventually take the Goldsmith stake, but at the company's next AGM in June, Mr Jocelyn Hambro resigned from the chair of SIH to the accompaniment of a bland announcement which only partially concealed from a fascinated City the blinding row going on between the company and its bank.

With most of the cards now face up on the table, the ritual pre-bid jostling for position began to take place. Having rejected the suggestion that Hilmar Reksten and Hambros director Ray Wheeler should join the board, the SIH directors laid themselves in battle array. Their first concern was to keep in close touch with any share movements, to keep internal morale high and the share price higher. If in the meantime it was possible to cast a little doubt on the opposition, then so much the better.

It was more than convenient that Jocelyn Hambro chose the day of the AGM to contract a bad cold which kept him in bed. That left Peter Parker in the chair, and the share price reacted favourably to his comments that he could 'smell the brimstone of bidding in the air'.

The next immediate task was to appoint a new merchant bank, and SIH board's choice fell not surprisingly, on Charles Ball, managing director of the major City bank Klienwort Benson. As well as being probably the most experienced and respected takeover gladiator in the City, Ball was also merchant banker to another of Parker's companies, Rockware.

SIH's next move, a revaluation of its assets, was also a standard weapon from the bid defenders' armoury. The 1972 accounts had revealed a book value of £41 million gross assets. With the verification of two independent firms of shipbrokers, one in London and one in Oslo, a revaluation was produced of more than three times the book value, making the assets worth not far short of £6 per share.

In the meantime, away from public gaze, a bustling volume of activity was going on. Parker was determined to make it as difficult as possible for anyone, but especially Hambros, to take any further aggressive actions. 'I needed to tie their hands', he said. In order to do so he lobbied all of those people whom he thought could be of help: Lord Shawcross, chairman of the City Takeover Panel, and Sir Gordon Richardson, the governor of the Bank of England, were both sent voluminous briefs. Also kept closely in touch was Dr John Gilbert, Labour front-bench spokesman for economic affairs and a rising star in the Labour party, whose support was to prove valuable in the later proceedings.

Great efforts had been made throughout to keep morale high within the company, and as early as December 1972 senior directors and executives of the broking companies had been suggesting that in the event of an unwelcome bid they might decide to go it alone. This was clearly an attitude that could have disuasive effect upon any unwelcome bidder, and the board made great efforts to keep the strong team spirit alive. Meetings of directors were held every morning and the managing director David Gault produced a special daily bulletin to keep everyone within the company in touch with events. Key journalists were also briefed on a regular and confidential basis, and on the Sunday after the AGM the *Sunday Telegraph's* top investigative financial reporter, Melvyn Marckus, revealed the extent of the acrimony between SIH and Hambros in an article entitled 'SIH – The anatomy of a blazing row'.

It now looked inevitable that a bid would come from someone at sometime, so rather than sit back and wait for a possible unwelcome suitor the board began to cast around for someone with whom they could happily go into harness. Opening moves were made, but before anything concrete could be decided upon the inevitable happened.

For some time Keith Wickenden, the chairman of European Ferries, had been building up a stake in SIH. Wickenden was not a dealer of the ilk of Slater or Goldsmith; he was a successful cross-channel ferry operator, but his company had its own problems in the shape of the Channel Tunnel which threatened to play havoc with his business if it ever came to be built. Wickenden was looking for a diversification, and SIH looked a real possibility. By October 1973 he had just under 10 per cent of the company and even at the then prevailing market price of 400p was sitting on a dealing profit which was beginning to be more tempting to him than the prospect of ownership of the company. He was not impressed by SIH's own valuation of £6 a share: 'value is one thing, what you can get in the market is quite another', he was reported as saying. When therefore he was offered what seemed like a top price of 450p for his stake he was only too keen to sell.

The buyer was a consortium consisting of the Vlasov Group, a privately controlled shipping group based in Monte Carlo, and Capitalfin International, itself a consortium registered in the Bahamas and owned jointly by the foreign subsidiaries of six of Italy's most powerful banking, financial and industrial companies. Boris Vlasov, head of the Vlasov Group and owner of a fleet itself said to be worth over £100 million at the time, was described in the press as 'a retiring White Russian *émigré*, now of Italian nationality'. All in all the Vlasov consortium, as it came to be known, paid £10.5 million for a 14.5 per cent stake in SIH, 9 per cent coming from Mr Wickenden through the good offices of City merchant bankers, S. G. Warburg, and the rest of the money came 'from other market sources'.

Vlasov's choice of City allies fell on the Drayton Group, in the dapper shape of Philip Shelbourne, backed up by the might of Lloyds and Bolsa. It was clear from the outset that a full-scale takeover bid was to be expected. Describing SIH as a 'beautiful company', Mr Shelbourne was reported as saying: 'the emphasis is to secure an agreed bid but a contested offer cannot be ruled out'.

On 7 November 1973 the Vlasov consortium finally cast its die by purchasing a total of 35 per cent of SIH, taking its holding up to more than 50 per cent, and created itself an obligation under Rule 35 of the City Takeover Code for an unconditional offer to be made to the remaining shareholders of SIH at the top price paid within the past twelve months. That price was 525p, valuing SIH at £83 million, almost three times the value that had been placed on the Group in the Stock Market just a year earlier.

SIH's fate was now to all intents and purposes sealed. The Vlasov consortium had 51 per cent of the equity and City commentators assumed that the fight was at last over. But not Parker and his board: SIH should not go to a foreign company, they said, and they said it loudly to anyone they thought could help; from the Italian ambassador in London, with the help of SIH director Sir Patrick Reilly; to Sir Geoffrey Howe, the minister of trade and consumer affairs; Peter Walker, the secretary of state for trade and industry; and Anthony Barber, the chancellor of the exchequer, all of the latter with the help of Dr John Gilbert.

Hambros was given a particularly rough ride by Dr Gilbert. In various questions levelled at government ministers, he called for the Bank's suspension from the Accepting Houses Committee under the bank of England Act of 1946 for having been involved in a major conflict-of-interest situation twice in three years. He also suggested in Parliament that it should be made a criminal offence for directors of financial institutions to fail to disclose to the boards of companies for which they act as advisers that they were seeking to arrange a warehousing operation in the shares of those companies.

In the many meetings that were taking place between the two sides, Charles Ball was emerging as the perfect foil to Philip Shelbourne. His phlegmatic calm and stolid insistence on a higher price for his clients so infuriated Drayton's Philip Shelbourne that for a time he would not even talk to Mr Ball. In the press questions were being asked about a foreign company gaining the access to UK tax concessions for shipowners, and elsewhere directors of the shipbroking and insurance companies were looking energetically around for a way out of the company. An elaborate contingency plan was laid which would have, at least in theory, enabled the brokers to move away from SIH if they could not have come to terms with Vlasov.

In the closing days of November the Vlasov Group bought another 10 per cent of the equity bringing its total up to 61 per cent; but still the SIH board held out. Keeping a close eye on the stock market to make sure that the share price did not fall too far below the 525p bid price, thus inhibiting the consortium from picking up too much cheap stock, they made the first ever application of its kind to the newly formed Office of Fair Trading (OFT) in an attempt to stop the bid.

The attempt failed, but a valuable concession was gained through the mediation of the OFT. Almost unbelievably, with 61 per cent of the equity, the Vlasov consortium agreed to raise its bid by 35p a share and further to guarantee to hive-off the shipbroking and insurance broking activities of the Group into a separate company which would retain the H. Clarkson name.

And in retrospect SIH shareholders did very well. By the middle of 1974 the shipping market was beginning to look decidedly soggy and rates had fallen substantially from their peak of a year before. The market has not yet recovered.

Of itself, the SIH defence was a masterpiece carried out against literally overwhelming odds at a time when the company was at its most vulnerable. The directors were fortunate in their main protagonists and used them well. Their success owed much to Charles Ball's impeccable tactics – 'always hold an argument or two back' – and Peter Parker's leadership, contacts and ability to phrase an argument well. But perhaps most of all, it owed a debt to the SIH management's determination, first to preserve the autonomy of the insurance and shipbroking operations, and more generally not to be taken for granted.

They fought back and carried on fighting to an unique finish, but equally importantly, they also knew when to call it a day. There is a price for every share, and the SIH board did not fall into the trap of allowing their desires to win to become obsessive, unlike some bid defenders whose prayer might have been that of the formidable Scottish priest: 'O Lord we pray we are right because we are verra, verra determined.'

If a checklist of rules for a defender were to be drawn up from the SIH directors' experiences, it might go as follows:

1. Know your price and be realistic.
2. Choose carefully those with whom you lodge your trust.
3. Know your audiences, government, shareholders, the press, your work force and maybe your trade and suppliers. See how they interrelate, and communicate with them, well and regularly.
4. Be alert to movements in ownership of your shares. Analyse share purchases and apply your best brains to the detective work of identifying the names behind nominee holdings.
5. Keep internal morale high. Communicate with the top executives and, at least, by daily briefing note, with everyone else. Do not leave workers to discover what is going on as best they can from the newspapers.

It may be this last point that will be of greatest importance in the future. The factor of worker and management reaction to takeover can no longer be ignored as largely it was in that period of most frenzied merger activity, called by Peter Parker, 'the mergerous sixties'.

21

Corporate Advocacy I

Virtually no company has decided to speak up in its own defence so extensively and with such resolve as Mobil Oil Corporation. In addition to challenging its critics, especially in the media, and enhancing its public reputation, Mobil wanted to contribute positively to the public debate on energy. The resulting communication programme, costing an estimated $12 million per year, began in the United States in 1973. Success there in its first few years has encouraged Mobil to move selected elements of the programme into Europe, starting initially in Britain.

In this case-study, Mobil Vice President Herbert Schmertz outlines the programme and gives examples of how his company has dealt with what it considers to be 'shoddy, misleading and just plain inaccurate' reporting.

In the United States, public opinion often dictates the political climate in which businesses must operate. Therefore, Mobil Oil Corporation decided some years ago to take part in the debates which help form public opinion – to inform people about issues crucial to both our corporation and our country.

We recognized that the United States was entering a period of energy shortage, and that unless oil companies were willing to speak out they would become prime targets of criticism from politicians and others.

In retrospect, our decision was a correct one, and we are proud of the success our public affairs efforts have had.

Ours is a two-pronged approach. It involves television and print.

The former includes our underwriting of cultural events and public television programmes. We felt, and still feel, that in the long term our company can function better in an environment characterized by informed rationality and sensitivity towards the arts and humanities. And we wanted to maintain and extend the reputation for quality that Mobil had built for more than a century – because we consider that reputation to be one of our prime business assets.

Other companies have underwritten public television productions, but it is safe to say that none has regularly matched the promotional efforts that Mobil has put behind its shows. We did more than underwrite 'Masterpiece Theatre'; we promoted it heavily and effectively, to the point where it has attracted one of the largest audiences in the history of public television.

In commercial television, we seek the same level of quality achieved in our Public Broadcasting Service offerings. But because of the dearth of high-quality network material available, we were unable to do as much commercial television as we would have liked – until early 1977. Then, we entered the non-network syndication field with 'Ten Who Dared', a series of hour-long programmes recreating the journeys of ten of the world's great explorers.

Mobil, in keeping with its custom, placed a heavy emphasis on promoting the series. It was shown in forty-three of the United States' largest television markets and, with few exceptions, was aired at the same time on the same evening. Thus, a network *effect* was created, which we will attempt to duplicate in future ventures into commercial television.

Through developing our own 'network', the unnecessarily tight control the major networks exercise over programming might be broken. We would like to contribute to opening up the airwaves to a greater variety and quality of programming. And we would like to see commercial time opened up to messages on issues vital to the future of the United States.

Currently, the networks reject advertising material on any subject they consider controversial. Mobil, for example, has been refused access to present messages on the energy situation – even when we made an unprecedented offer to purchase equal time for those whose views might differ from ours. The networks feel that energy is an issue that should be handled solely by their news departments. And television news, because of the limitations of time, is notoriously inadequate when it comes to covering complex issues. A thirty-second segment on a news programme, or even an hour-long special, is simply insufficient coverage of an issue such as energy – especially if oil companies, which have the greatest expertise in the area, are accorded little or no chance for meaningful input.

Mobil hoped to contribute to the national debate on energy through commercial messages. In one commercial we prepared, the camera would have focused on a beach while the announcer said:

> According to the US Geological Survey, there may be sixty billion barrels of oil or more beneath our continental shelves.
>
> Some people say we should be drilling for that oil. Others say we shouldn't because of the possible environmental risks. We'd like to know what you think.
>
> Write Mobil Poll, Room 647, 150 East 42 Street, New York, New York 10017.
>
> We'd like to hear from you.

The reaction to that harmless commercial illustrates the arbitrary nature of the networks' use of their tremendous power. NBC accepted it without change; ABC rejected it without explanation; and CBS turned it down because it dealt 'with a controversial issue of public importance'.

That brought out the combative side of Mobil's public affairs operations – the willingness to 'trade punches', as *Fortune* put it. In a newspaper ad, we reproduced the commercial message and the networks' replies. More than 2,000 persons responded to the ad, and the overwhelming majority – by 70 per cent to 12 per cent – favoured our right to express our viewpoint on the air.

It is not only the networks' stubborn refusal to loosen their grip on commercial time that has put Mobil in toe-to-toe battle with television; we are also not hesitant to take issue with the contents of television's reporting on energy, when we believe the reporting is shoddy, misleading, or just plain inaccurate.

A case in point is the feud that erupted in 1976 between Mobil and WNBC-TV, the New York outlet for the national network. The station announced that it would run a series titled 'The Great Gasoline War' on its 6 pm news show during the week of 23-27 February 1976.

Because of previous disappointments with television news shows in which interviews of thirty minutes or more were edited down to one- or two-minute segments – which sometimes bore little or no relation to the point Mobil wanted to make – we have avoided participating in such interviews. Thus, when invited by WNBC-TV to take part, we declined. We did not, however, let the show pass unnoticed, but closely monitored its entire run.

The very first segment showed that our concerns were well founded. The series was so full of distortions and errors – including the old myth about tankers waiting off the coast until prices rose – that we knew we would have to reply. The rest of the week, Mobil's staff monitored the series and developed responses. A full-page newspaper ad was written over the weekend, and management reviews were obtained early the following week. The result was a full-page ad which ran in the *New York Times* on Friday, 5 March. The following Monday it appeared in the *New York Daily News* and in the eastern edition of The *Wall Street Journal.*

The ad, titled 'Whatever happened to fair play?', called the WNBC programme 'inaccurate, unfair, and a disservice to the people', and 'a parade of warmed-over distortions, half-truths, and down-right untruths marching across the screen like an army of tired ghosts – ghosts we thought had been laid to rest two years ago'.

The ad provided details on what we labelled 'hatchet jobs', and a small drawing of a hatchet accompanied each distortion. Among the distortions – and Mobil's responses:

HATCHET JOB: At the outset, Ms Trotta (the narrator) referred to 'the rather vague circumstances that surrounded the Arab oil embargo back in 1973'.

FACT: There wasn't anything 'vague' about the embargo. The Arab nations made a simple straightforward decision to use oil as a political weapon and they cut off supplies to certain countries, including the United States. We hope Liz Trotta knew this. If she didn't, her research was shoddy. Apparently she preferred to create an aura of mystery and conspiracy around a straightforward set of circumstances.

HATCHET JOB: Said Ms Trotta: 'The objective, then, is to sell as much gasoline as possible to keep the high-profit refining operation going'.

FACT: What high profit? Mobil's US refining and marketing operations actually lost money in 1974 and began to break even only in 1975.

HATCHET JOB: This one is a beauty, because it involved television production technique, rather than words alone. Says a dealer: 'The only difference between them [oil companies] and the hoodlums in the street is that they don't get caught. They're too big.' Then the camera flashes back to an oil company executive, obviously in the midst of a prerecorded interview, and the first words allowed to come out of his mouth are: 'It is true, we're not willing to subsidize an economic loss at a marginal station . . . .'

FACT: The implication is clear. The oil man is made to appear in agreement with the line about 'hoodlums'. Frankly, nothing in the show made us as angry as that cheap distortion, because it was so patently contrived.

Mobil also sent a letter to the station offering to purchase a half hour of time to 'present additional information which we feel is pertinent to the many issues raised by Ms Trotta'.

WNBC-TV disagreed with our ad, rejected our request, and countered with an offer to allow a company spokesperson to air a brief statement, after which he would respond to a series of questions posed by Ms Trotta.

Mobil refused that offer, calling it,

'patently unfair because it would be impossible for Mobil to compress its response into a short statement of a few minutes in reply to five nights of one-sided editorializing totaling some thirty-six minutes.

Second, the format you offer is irresponsible because it exacerbates the unfairness of the original show, in which WNBC-TV News and Ms Trotta used their full control over the structure of the show to present a biased report on the complex issues involved. Mobil does not believe it can redress this unfair presentation with WNBC-TV News controlling the agenda of the questions posed by Ms Trotta.

The letter concluded with a repeated request for unedited time.

Mobil had two goals in mind in responding to the series. First, we wanted to set the record straight. Second, we wanted to put the media on notice that somebody was watching and was ready to point out their mistakes.

We think we achieved a significant victory. *Time* and *Newsweek* ran generally favourable articles, as did many other publications. Even Milton Moskowitz, a tough consumer advocate, noted in his *San Francisco Examiner* column: 'It's nothing short of amazing that only one company seems to know how to fight back against critics.'

The furor prompted WNBC to schedule another energy special on 15 May, in which Mobil and two other industry representatives participated, along with three critics.

In both our battle with the networks over access to commercial time and our correction of the distortions in the WNBC-TV series, Mobil reached its audience effectively through the print media. It has been our general experience that it is more effective to communicate through magazines and newspapers, and we have been extremely active in this area since we first made the decision to speak out. In 1970, The *New York Times* opened up a quarter of its 'opposite-editorial' page to advertising. It was an opportunity Mobil quickly seized, and our messages have been appearing weekly in that newspaper. The 'opposite-editorial' pieces cover a wide range of serious topics. Our first one, for instance, spoke out forcefully for improved public transportation.

In addition to the *New York Times,* Mobil's 'opposite-editorial' messages run in the *Washington Post,* the *Wall Street Journal, Chicago Tribune, Los Angeles Times* and the *Boston Globe* on a regular basis. And at the height of the 1973-74 oil embargo, they appeared weekly in more than 100 papers.

The 'opposite-editorial' messages are supplemented by another print campaign: Mobil's 'Observations' column. 'Observations' is a flexible, chatty, sometimes irreverent collection of short features stressing company viewpoints and discussing general concerns of the people. One item might discuss the need for offshore drilling, and be followed by an item on the costs of sending our children to college.

By running the column in the Sunday magazines – *Parade, Family Weekly,* the *New York Times Sunday Magazine* and a number of other Sunday supplements, 'Observations' reaches 45 per cent of all American households. About 30,000 letters were generated by the column in 1976 and the readership scores for 'Observations' were the highest in *Parade's* history for half-page black-and-white ads.

Mobil's print efforts have increased and expanded the public debate on issues that are crucial to the future of our nation – and we are prepared to contribute via television, as soon as that medium accepts the responsibility of its role as the most popular communications device ever developed.

Yet, our efforts go beyond buying space and trying to purchase air time. Mobil also does a great deal of talking directly to newsmen. We regularly play host to editorial staffs of key publications at media luncheons in our headquarters, for example, and most of our top people have been on media tours. In a typical tour, one of our executives will visit a city, meeting the editorial boards of the leading newspapers and appearing on two or three television or radio shows. Between 1975 and 1977 Mobil executives ranging from our chairman, Rawleigh Warner, Jr, to key managers in our US Division talked to newspeople at some eighty papers and appeared on over 200 radio and 360 television programmes. Additionally, we have a speaker's programme in which some 100 other employees speak to community groups such as Rotary Clubs.

Mobil believes that, while the media have a duty to be responsible and to present a variety of opinions on serious issues, the private sector also has a duty. Businesses must make themselves accessible if they are going to demand access; they must contribute to public understanding if they are going to request public support.

In the United States Mobil has a well-earned reputation for speaking out on behalf of private enterprise, of protecting the interests of our company and our shareholders against attacks from those who seek to solve serious problems by rhetoric and irrational proposals.

Overseas Mobil is also extremely active in public relations activities. Our affiliates have sponsored cultural events such as festivals and art shows, and run a number of community programmes. They, like those of us in the United States, feel it is important to make positive contributions to the countries and communities in which Mobil does business.

The corporate public relations department supports Mobil's overseas efforts wherever we can. Books have been produced as lasting mementos of the cultural events underwritten by our affiliates. A poster exhibit – 'Images of an Era' – that Mobil sponsored as part of the American Bicentennial was taken to Europe, and hosted by our affiliates in the various countries in which it was shown. And *Pegasus,* a Mobil-produced publication that makes little or no reference to the company, is circulated on a world-wide basis to a limited audience.

Our experience in corporate advertising – gained in the United States through our 'opposite-editorial' messages and the like – enabled us to introduce Mobil to the British public. Although Mobil is a major participant in North Seas oil exploration, we were a relatively unknown company in the United Kingdom – until the autumn of 1976. We began at the time to run a series of full-page ads in leading newspapers in England and Scotland. The typical ad included a picture of a British oil worker in the North Sea, with the text being a brief profile of the worker and an explanation of Mobil's involvement in North Sea petroleum development.

Mobil is a successful, concerned corporation – we would be less than responsible to our shareholders and to the countries in which we operate if we were not. And Mobil is intent on having its voice heard on the critical issues of the day – we would be less than responsible as a corporate citizen if we were not.

Our public relations activities are geared toward assuring a climate in which we can continue to make both profits and contributions.

22

Corporate Advocacy II

At the beginning of the 1970s ITT, the American multinational, headed into a series of political controversies that earned it front-page headlines throughout the world. Stories about the company (from being accused of trying to prevent the election of Marxist Salvador Allende as president of Chile to securing favours from the Nixon Administration) had all the drama and spice of good fiction. In Europe, as elsewhere, their impact was dramatic. Factories and offices were bombed, recruiters from ITT subsidiaries were hounded off university campuses, employee morale was depressed, and there was outright hostility in some government circles.

How should a company like ITT respond in such a situation, if at all?

This case-study, by co-author Nigel Rowe, looks at how ITT became a target for corporate abuse, what the corporation did about it in Europe, and how successful it was. From 1971 to 1976 Nigel Rowe was on the staff of ITT Europe, the last four years of which as assistant director for public relations.

During the first half of this decade not more than one European in fifty had ever heard of ITT. The company had deliberately maintained a 'low profile' in Europe. By 1973, however, an estimated one in five

Europeans knew the company, and virtually the only things 95 per cent of these knew were the accusations against it.

Quite apart from the accuracy or otherwise of the accusations (and ITT eventually denied every one of them, with varying degrees of success), the corporation had contributed inadvertently to its own demise in Europe by presenting a very easy target for critics of the multinational corporation.It will be remembered that ITT's troubles coincided with, and in part created, the height of the debate on multinationals in the early 1970s. The reasons why ITT was such an easy target contain lessons for other companies to learn from today.

In the 1960s it had been ITT policy to permit the management of subsidiary companies to decide largely for themselves whether or not to identify publicly with the parent corporation, based on the perceived commercial needs of each company. Very few chose to do so. One of the results was the creation of an 'information gap' of considerable proportions between the corporation and the outside world, a vacuum into which accusation and innuendo was poured and automatically rendered credible. The problem was summed up well by a senior official at the EEC Commission in 1973 who said: 'Most people know so little about ITT in Europe, except that you are so big and powerful, that it is hardly surprising you are mistrusted. If the facts were known perhaps people would feel differently about you.'

ITT is a very large company with a broadly diversified range of products and services, operating in all five continents. It is a complex organization and it takes a great deal of time to understand it. Its management style since the early 1960s has been essentially pragmatic, with emphasis on maximization of profit. It was also somewhat decentralized. Until recently a great deal of autonomy, especially in the non-commercial areas, was vested in local management. Because of this individual subsidiaries retained their own individual characters and public identities. Most of them were not associated in people's minds with ITT, and to those who did know ITT, its reputation was that of an aggressively managed, financially oriented corporation. Indeed, this was the thrust of ITT's very limited corporate public relations effort in Europe during the 1960s.

These factors, coupled with a lack of public knowledge of ITT's broader corporate character in Europe and its real social and economic impact on the countries in which it operated, provided fertile soil for hostility – a breeding ground for suspicion and accusation. This was especially true in the political context of Europe in the 1970s. The need for some action was obvious, and the necessity of more effective communication a first essential.

Since 1969 the corporation had sponsored annual research into attitudes towards business, multinationals and ITT, and it was therefore in a good position to track trends and spot some of the emerging problems. With the help of this research the company was able to ascertain the main facets of its corporate image in Europe, both positive and negative. It was able to weigh each element to reflect its importance and relevance to those with whom the company sought to communicate (for example, export performance, balance of payments impact, investments, employment and contributions to technology were among those identified as being highly relevant to varying degrees across Europe). The degree of interest in individual issues varied enormously from country to country, however. Indeed, one of the early lessons to be learned was that there could be no tidy pan-European communication programme.

Identification of whom the company should communicate with was determined at an early stage. The priorities were: opinion-leading segments of government, the civil service and the professions, business leaders, the media, and the company's own employees. It was felt that a broader definition of the 'target audience' would lead to confusion and conflict in programme-planning and unacceptably high costs. A maximum budget of $1.2 million had been set for 1974, the first year any communication programme could be run.

It was also recognized that, within this definition of whom the company wanted to communicate with there would be those, especially on the political Left, who would remain unshakeably negative towards ITT as (in their eyes) a leading exponent of brash American-style capitalism. Equally, there would be those at the other end of the spectrum who would be positive toward ITT for exactly the same reasons. It was decided therefore to concentrate on those that fell between these two extremes.

Five central programmes were developed as the communication vehicles, each with distinctively different characteristics that collectively would perform like one of those twenty-four-hour cold cure capsules which contain separate ingredients taking effect with different intensities at different times. In addition to the five central programmes executed largely by ITT Europe from its Brussels headquarters, there were two additional elements left squarely in the hands of local subsidiary managements – contact with national government officials and communication with employees. On this local management insisted.

The five central elements of the programme were:

1. a comprehensive 'fact file' on ITT in Europe, published in several languages;
2. a new quarterly external magazine, also published in several languages;
3. a speakers' programme.
4. a comprehensive press relations programme;
5. corporate advertising campaigns in key national markets.

In many respects the first of these programmes, titled *Facts about ITT in Europe*, was the cornerstone of the whole programme package in that it was a first demonstration of the corporation's willingness to talk about almost every aspect of its operation and impact in Europe. Published in six separate language editions (English, German, French, Spanish, Italian and Dutch), and destined to become an annual publication, it was immediately acclaimed as being widely responsive to the public demand that multinational corporations should be more open about who and what they are. The first edition of the 'fact file' contained a great deal of previously unpublished material and detailed the company's history, policy and structure in Europe as well as profiling its eight key areas of business activity. It also contained detailed statistics on ITT in Europe covering number of employees (on a country-by-country basis), salaries, wages, taxes, social contributions, dividends, research and capital investment expenditures, etc. It was first published in 1974 and has since been distributed to more than 100,000 of the target audience throughout Europe annually. The cost of the twenty-page publication remains less than $0.50 per copy.

The primary objective of the quarterly external magazine, titled *Profile* (because this was one of the few words that worked well in the five languages in which it was published), was to help create a better understanding of ITT's corporate character in Europe and to detail some of its practical achievements and contributions to the countries and communities affected by the corporation's activities in Europe. It was also designed to be a positive contribution to the broader debate on the multinational corporation. It was decided that the editorial mix of the magazine should be a subtle blend of fact and comment on ITT in Europe, leavened with some 60 per cent of general interest feature material on such issues as worker participation, European culture, management techniques and social responsibility. Each issue contained a story with real news value, and considerable effort was devoted to generating publicity for the magazine and its content in key national newspapers and magazines. Initial distribution to a list of 55,000, which took more than six months to develop, has now climbed to nearly 90,000 per issue. The cost of the magazine, including distribution, is still below $1 per copy.

For the speaker's programme, the European public relations team developed original speech material on a range of subjects including aspects of the multinational corporation, youth and business, and social responsibility. It also developed a special three-day course in public speaking for senior executives at ITT Europe headquarters who had been identified as a 'Speakers Panel'.

The overall public relations effort placed considerable emphasis on a corporate press relations activity on two counts. First, the press had been highly critical of ITT, and at first the corporation had let virtually all the accusations against it go unchallenged. The chief reason for this was said at the time to be due to pending litigation related to US Congressional hearings and a $90 million insurance claim following expropriation of company facilities in Chile, both factors placing constraints on the company in making public statements on the key issues. However, considerable internal pressure built up in Europe calling for action of some kind – 'if the charges are untrue, deny them publicly'. As a result, virtually every piece of unjustified press coverage was challenged and rebutted in Europe from that time on – an activity that was at least 75 per cent successful in its demand for published corrections. Second, the company in Europe decided to adopt a new open-door policy with the media, making its top management in Brussels and in subsidiary companies much more available for journalists to interview. It also sponsored a series of European tours of its facilities and research establishments for key European journalists. Considerable and favourable press coverage resulted. The cost of the press relations programme was mostly that of executive time, since travel and related costs were minimal in the context of the overall communication programme.

By far the most visible and dramatic programme in the overall package, however, was the corporate advertising campaign. Four basic 'messages' had been identified for each of ITT's six major national markets in Europe, each reflecting the interests and issues of concern in each country. But designing the vehicle to carry the message was where the fun started. In Britain, where the campaign was first developed, seven different versions were created and tested before the right solution was found. The campaign that researched the best was the simplest in terms of creativity, and used the fewest words to present each message. The advertisements covered whole-page spaces in the 'quality' newspapers and two-page spreads in magazines. Half the space was given over to headlines like 'Who the devil does ITT think it is?' and 'Does ITT give a damn about Britain's balance of payments?', and the other half to about 200 words of fact and statistics. Research indicated that a similar approach might work in other countries too, except for what the advertising agency called its 'tone of voice'. In France and Spain, for example, the bold and aggressive headlines received a very negative reaction when tested. A much softer and subtler approach was called for. Planned annual costs for each national advertising campaign ranged from $200,000 in Britain to $400,000 in Germany.

Probably no part of the overall communication programme would have been implemented if it had not been for a broad measure of European management involvement in its development and support in its executions. This was especially true of the corporate press relations programme and advertising campaign (a second phase of which has already run in Britain, and a third is being developed). Senior management involvement began with two eight-hour meetings attended by the corporation's top twenty European managers and the two most senior relations specialists from ITT Europe headquarters. The sole purpose of the first of these meetings was to discuss the communication problem in Europe, its source and impact, and decide whether or not to do anything about it. The second was to agree on a basic strategy for action which the public relations team would translate into an action plan. The decision to take action was therefore the result of a full understanding by management of the character of the problem and its effect on a range of company activities including sales, government relations and recruitment, not to mention the morale of present employees. This meant that once the action plan had been developed its implementation had the full weight and impetus of management support behind it.

So how successful has ITT's communication programme package for Europe been since its launch in late 1974?

In the first place, it won extensive praise in the press and elsewhere. It has been featured as case-study material in communication textbooks and has been used as public relations/advertising/marketing case-study material by several universities and management schools. When it was first launched, Britain's *Financial Times* predicted the programme 'could have a significant influence on the thinking of other multinationals'. The ITT Europe programme has subsequently had its imitators.

Much more important than this for ITT, however, has been the impact of the programme on those whose opinions it had been planned to influence. Until 1977 Britain was the only country in Europe to feel the full weight of the entire programme package. Predictably, it was there that the most dramatic shifts in attitudes towards ITT were registered. In its opinion research programme ITT measures attitudes towards itself against attitudes towards IBM and Philips (respectively an American and European multinational). While the attitude towards these two companies remained fairly level over the period 1971-75 (when the ITT campaign moved into top gear), attitudes towards ITT measured on the same basis rose sharply after a sudden dip from 1971 to 1973. A similar but much less dramatic story held true for other European countries.

While four of the five key programmes have been implemented in most of Europe, by 1977 the advertising campaign had been run only in Britain. Complete campaigns were developed and ready to run in other countries; but in the case of France, for example, the decision to publish was delayed for so long that it was overtaken by events. (In 1975 the company was forced into protracted and delicate negotiations with the French government, resulting in the sale of ITT's largest French company, and it was considered to be the wrong time to indulge in such an overt form of communication as corporate advertising.) In Spain the campaign was about to be launched when General Franco died, plunging the country into political turmoil – again, not the right environment for a company like ITT to use a communication instrument as blunt and heavy as corporate advertising.

ITT managers in Europe are under no illusions as to the magnitude of the task that still lies ahead in rehabilitating ITT's corporate image. Plans are being made to run the corporate advertising campaign in other countries, and to expand other elements of the overall programme, notably in the area of press relations. While its critics claim that more fundamental change in corporate policy and behaviour will be necessary for it to achieve complete corporate respectability, ITT believes that the problem will be solved by bridging the 'information gap', a task that it knows will require continuous long-term action.

SECTION FIVE

The future for free enterprise and how industry can improve its prospects

23. The Future for Free Enterprise

23

The Future for Free Enterprise

Any forecast as to what will happen in Europe must be based on what has happened already, and we have to recognize at the outset that the course of events has not been the same in north and south. In the north the progress of socialism has centred upon workers' participation, upon recognizing the internationalism of trade, resisting the large-scale nationalization of industry and in some cases upon avoiding statutory price and wage control. Socialism in the north has created some measure of political and industrial stability with all the inherent strength that must result from an essentially democractic structure. The populations of the northern countries, notably Scandinavia and Germany, are better educated and more responsible. They are unlikely to move further to the left because the more divisive aspects of society, in so far as they ever existed, have mostly disappeared. The demand for equality has been more or less satisfied and the current movement is rather in the other direction. With its momentum gone, as the penalty of success, socialism has come to be regarded as rather a bore. Free enterprise would seem to have a future in these countries, more especially as linked with industrial democracy. Norway and Sweden are particularly fortunate in their low population density and lack of huge industrial cities. They have a material basis for democratic stability.

The situation in southern Europe, in Italy for example, and in Spain and Portugal, is entirely different. Many southern populations were quite primitive within living memory, have only recently become literate and have little grasp of economic or political realities. Sharp divisions between rich and poor are reflected in bad relations between management and labour. There is an eager public for drastic solutions and violent proposals. Half of Italian industry is already state-owned and a third of the electorate voted communist in 1976. The recent success of the Socialist–Communist alliance in France has been considerable and would seem to foreshadow a possible triumph in the general election due to take place in 1978.

But while there is a contrast between north and south, which may also reflect a contrast between Protestant and Catholic, we do well to remember that there are sharp differences within the national boundaries. In Italy, the industrial cities of Milan and Turin have little in common with Naples or Sicily. Northern and southern Portugal are almost as distinct from each other as Andalusia and Catalonia. France itself is not as unified as its centralized structure would lead us to suppose. There are great dangers in making any predictions that will apply to Europe as a whole.

To add still more to the complexities of the situation, the United Kingdom refuses to fit into the general pattern. The socialist movement there has lost its momentum, for reasons that are fairly easy to understand. Many of the original objectives of the political Left have been achieved, leaving the reformers to make demands that are increasingly controversial. Past schemes of nationalization have not been spectacularly successful, least of all in preventing industrial dispute. People are also beginning to realize that socialism is more readily workable in a communist form and that communism means the loss of freedom. Politically, British socialism is lacking in inspiration. Intellectually, it has come to a grinding halt. There might be, in theory, a reaction from groups that seek to recover and retain freedom – freedom of enterprise, freedom from bureaucracy, freedom from governmental interference. But parties of the Right have also tended to lose their appeal, in part perhaps through supporting policies that derive from the Left. Britain seems, therefore, to offer a special case. Its social and industrial structure is one reminiscent, perhaps, of southern Europe; its national and cultural background is that of the north. It has the most powerful and antiquated trades union movement in Europe, militant in its support of the most outmoded dogmas and loud in its condemnation of evils that often no longer exist. In Britain, too, there are significantly different trends in north and south, in Lancashire and Wessex, in Cornwall and Wales. It does not offer us a subject for easy generalities.

In so far as generalization is possible, we may conclude that socialism has lost its momentum in northern Europe and that the future would seem to offer a field for compromise. Free enterprise can flourish, we may conclude, alongside industries that have been nationalized, and it has a still brighter future if modified by the concept of industrial democracy. The picture in southern Europe is not as hopeful so far as the immediate future is concerned. The attempt to introduce sophisticated industries among unsophisticated peoples must produce real problems and would seem to involve some very real dangers. Things are made worse when reformers seek to apply the same sort of theological beliefs to a wide variety of political and economic situations. If we are all more or less agreed on wanting people to have happier and more prosperous lives in better surroundings, we can argue rationally about the best way to bring this about. We can, in these circumstances, point to past experiments and current statistics, dealing with figures and quoting ascertainable facts. We find it more difficult to argue with people whose aims are entirely distinct and who are indifferent to any measurable achievement. There are folk whose standards of excellence are solely based on what Karl Marx said in 1848. Such theological concepts are not very consistent with rational argument and still less, perhaps, with material progress. The future would thus seem to offer both difficulties and dangers. It also offers, however, a great opportunity.

We have seen that some northern countries have reached an apparently stable solution of the problem of how to integrate industry with democracy. This solution depends upon two major assumptions: first, that the industry is profitable, and second that the employees are not seeking red revolution for its own sake. Elsewhere these two conditions are absent and the same solution is not easy to apply. So the Mediterranean countries are tending towards more extreme remedies for their real or imagined ills. The objection to the 'northern' pattern of compromise is that the resulting way of life is apt to be dull and that its mere dullness may produce an eventual revolt. The objection to the 'southern' pattern of revolutionary fervour is that it must tend to produce dictatorship and cannot possibly produce anything else. Socialism in that form is perfectly workable as from the moment when democracy is abolished. Nor can it be doubted that great achievements can result from it. Men who were idle can be made to work. Men who were dishonest can be transformed into models of reliability. Great schemes of construction can be completed on schedule. All that has been lost is freedom, and about this only a few people will have any real regret. For the vast majority the things that matter are safety and order, shelter and food. Success in providing everyone with these necessities is not to be despised. This may not, however, be the sort of success we wish to emulate.

If our analysis is correct, it might seem that Europe has a choice between the 'northern' and 'southern' types of industrial regime; and most readers would probably agree that the 'northern' compromise seems preferable. We should, however, remember that all variants on the socialist or semi-socialist theme are open to one serious objection. They invariably leave too little scope for imagination. The industries that we have brought under democratic control, deploring as we do so the evils of capitalism, were themselves created by men of imagination in a free environment. It is simple for an enlightened regime to nationalize the motor industry and bring workers into the management. But if we suppose, as we must, that the motorcar is obsolescent, that the internal combustion engine is too costly to run and that something entirely different is to take its place, we need a new Gottlieb Daimler to invent it and a new Henry Ford to mass-produce it. We need individuals, in fact, who combine imagination with ability and determination. Are we likely to find them among the members of a semi-socialist cabinet? Should we be any more likely to find them among the members of an enlightened town council? The bureaucrats who devise systems of registration or taxation could never have created what they now seek to control. It is easy for us to shake our heads over the robber barons who figure in the industrial history of the United States, but the fact remains that they created the world in which we actually live. Our lives are shaped by Remington and Kellogg, by Boeing and Bell. Where are we to look for the ideas of the future? There were bankers in the past who would invest money in some new invention which would ruin an existing industry. How could a politician or civil servant find the courage to do that? And yet all the future of an industrial society must depend upon such decisions, taken by men who combine technical knowledge with imagination, foresight, resolution and ruthlessness.

To achieve some measure of industrial stability might not be too difficult, but how are we to ensure that we do not thereby establish industrial stagnation? Our aim in the welfare state is to maintain conditions that are fair to all. But are such conditions dynamic? Are they even as dynamic as the life-style to be found in Siberia? It is not enough, surely, to establish some compromise between socialism and capitalism, between the regimes set up in northern and southern Europe, between controlled capitalism and industrial democracy? In the Europe of the future we shall need somehow to combine the opposites, free enterprise and worker's participation, stability and dynamic change. Is this to ask the impossible? It might seem so, and yet it is also the minimum we must ask if an industrial society is to survive at all. It remains to see how we must set about it.

AN INDUSTRY RESPONSE

Industrialists who believe in free enterprise should advocate the unity of Europe so as to create a wider market. To make this advocacy effective, their first move should be to achieve unity among themselves. Were they to form, first of all, an Industrial Congress of Europe, comprising delegates from all the larger countries, they could jointly exercise a considerable influence on the national governments. If such a Congress were to meet each year and elect the members of a smaller Industrial Council, a new aspect would be added to the movement for European unity. All would depend, however, on the reputation gained by the Council for its public spirit, far-sightedness and enlightenment. It would be judged, inevitably, by its action against pollution of the air and water, the evil that is within the scope of industry to remedy and largely beyond the scope of any merely national government. As things stand the reputation of industry, and especially of big business, suffers from a criticism that fastens inevitably upon the destruction of the environment. Some dramatic moves to end the evils of pollution – except that caused by the governments themselves – would establish the Industrial Congress as a power in its own right and one that the politicians would have to respect. When the Parliament of Europe has gained greater authority it would be strengthened, not weakened, by the parallel existence of the Industrial Congress as a force for unity and one which will exercise a different kind of control.

If it is to survive, free enterprise must learn to communicate. Having found the necessary organization, the businessmen who seek to recover and retain freedom must learn to defend themselves, no longer allowing their case to go by default. We have seen in earlier chapters that leaders of industry are now aware of this. They are increasingly prepared for a wider and more vigorous effort in public relations. Their tendency, however, is to confine this effort to a narrow field, failing to reach sections of opinion that are important now and failing still more to reach the sections of public opinion that will be important in the future. The effort they will need to make must be redirected as well as intensified. The case for free enterprise must be illustrated by television programmes, by films, articles, books and lectures. There has been a tendency in the past for the industrial company to deploy some of these means in its own defence; but the case should be made for free enterprise as a whole and the case on that level is unanswerable. It would be wrong to argue that public ownership is inevitably disastrous. It is, however, quite safe to assert that the absence of free enterprise must mean ultimate suicide. How can any new device gain acceptance if the inventor is confronted only by bureaucrats, civil servants, trade union officials and the heads of nationalized industry? All these are the appointed guardians of an existing establishment, a public service and a closed shop. What the inventor needs is a group of men who are willing to take a risk, who care nothing about the vested interests and whose judgement is likely to be right. There have been instances, we know, of governments boldly taking a commercial risk, but they have almost invariably proved to be wrong. Risking other people's money is quite different, in fact, from risking your own.

Such a campaign for free enterprise would have to overcome a great deal of opposition. It would have to recapture a lot of ground that has been lost. It would meet with ignorance, suspicion and fear. It would have to win for industry a place in education, a share of television time and a fairer treatment in the press. In gaining attention, the representatives of industry must show a willingness to regulate their own trade practices and a readiness to co-operate with sensible legislation. They must reveal a sense of corporate social responsibility, showing real concern over working conditions, environmental issues and safety standards. Having done something to counteract the effect of bad publicity in the past, the defenders of free enterprise must next rid themselves of all taint of monopoly. Those who have been loudest in their praise for free competition have often been more quietly intent on limiting competition by amalgamation and by private agreement with supposedly rival firms. The competition we seek to defend and increase must be a reality, not a fiction. When all these precautions have been taken, the effort can be made to show all that private enterprise has achieved and can achieve again. Nor is it difficult to sustain the argument at this level, because the proofs of success are all about us. Our lives are shaped for us by the equipment we use. Without the products of private enterprise our society could not even exist.

In summary, then, businessmen should concentrate upon an improved standard of public relations. The aim should be to show that European industry is ahead of European politics, its leaders being more united, more imaginative, more disciplined and more determined. Given the right direction and using the right methods, the campaign we advocate would tend to establish the influence of European leaders of industry. It need hardly be added that a wrongly directed campaign would backfire in a damaging way, doing infinite harm to the cause it was planned to promote. So there is scope for more careful thought and for studying the techniques of diplomacy. Having said that, we must remember, however, that diplomacy is far removed from the popular conception of it. The diplomat is not a specialist in tactful misrepresentation. His task is rather to gain the confidence of ministers and other diplomats, using their trust as a basis for negotiation and so wording each document or telegram as to avoid all possibility of misinterpretation. The object must be to gain credibility and inspire trust, an object of which some corporations would seem to have lost sight. The fact is that the function in the world of a multinational company, which has been something of a mystery to politicians, has also puzzled the executives of the companies themselves. It is not surprising that some mistakes have been made, but the rules of the game are emerging in the course of play and we can fairly assume that they will be observed. It is the strength of the businessman that his view is increasingly international. Using that advantage, he can in time convince the politician that we must look beyond the views and aspirations of any one electorate. We must learn, in fact, to think as Europeans. There are those who will add that we must also think as democrats.

US investment in Europe is levelling off, and probably decreasing in real dollar terms. Indeed there is evidence of many US corporations leaving less of their European profits in local reserves and repatriating more as dividends to the parent company – preferring to finance local (European) investment through local borrowings. And with a greater repatriation of profits there has been an increase in the repatriation of management control.

The time has come for European industry to emerge from the Marshall Plan era and learn to stand more on its own two feet. This need not imply a conflict with the United States; but a more productive relationship could result from a greater European emancipation within the Western economic system. We also have to recognize some of the fundamental differences in the character, and to some extent in the priorities, of industrial enterprise in the two continents. For this to happen, however, there will need to be a revival of the European sense of unity, and a much greater sense of urgency behind efforts to create a genuine European economic community. This would result in a more fruitful partnership of the two economies and so avoid pressure from the political Left in Europe for a reduction of American influence.

It would certainly be to the long-term advantage of US business to encourage this process. Americans should accept Europe's industrial democracy rather than fight it. They should be more ready to share the ownership of their European businesses with local national investors to help protect their own long-term future as well as that of free enterprise in general. They should also expect and welcome a higher level of European investment in US industry. They should not wait for a European Declaration of Independence. Unlike King George III, they should yield a little before it is too late.

It is arguable, finally, that the solution of industrial problems in Europe may well be an example to the rest of the world. The problems of production in Russia and China have been at least partly solved by the sacrifice of freedom. The same problems have been more successfully solved in the United States by the sacrifice of federal competence and by some imbalance between social and economic objectives. Elsewhere, the gains in production have been a great deal less and the losses, whether of public order or of freedom, have been a great deal more. In Europe the opportunity exists to find the unique solution to problems that have been solved elsewhere, if at all, at too heavy a cost. In business, as in politics, the way to success must involve a reconciliation of forces that are apparently opposed. There must be unity without uniformity, diversity without fragmentation, order without tyranny, freedom without chaos. Is it really possible to achieve so fine a balance? It is probably more possible in Europe than anywhere else. In no other continent could one as readily assemble all that is needed in tolerance and foresight, in experience and in brains. As compared with many other people, businessmen have the advantage that they talk the same language and have had the same sort of training. Their contribution could therefore be of the greatest importance. They cannot contribute, however, until they have learnt to express themselves. It is now their cue to learn the arts of communication, assembling their facts, clarifying their views, reaching their conclusions and choosing their words. They must be literate as well as numerate, ready to take their place in the councils of Europe. In the past they have been merely consulted; in the future they must be ready to lead. But leadership involves, among other things, the ability to explain what has to be done. It implies the capacity to make oneself heard. Almost before anything else, the leader's duty is to *communicate*.